BLITZ
1940

KRIEG

WARD RUTHERFORD

GALLERY BOOKS
An imprint of W.H. Smith Publishers Inc.
112 Madison Avenue
New York, New York 10016

Published by Gallery Books
A Division of W H Smith Publishers Inc.
112 Madison Avenue
New York, New York 10016

Produced by
Brompton Books Corp.
15 Sherwood Place
Greenwich, CT 06830

ISBN 0-8317-0915-4

Printed in Hong Kong

9 8 7 6 5 4 3 2

Reprinted 1989

Contents

THANK GO FRENCH

Winston Churchill in conversation
with General Georges.

D FOR THE ARMY

The French Army prides itself on *vivacité militaire* — on a brisk and soldierly smartness about all it does. Its march tempo is a little quicker; the predominant sounds of its bands are those of trumpet and side-drum. Thus it was to this stirring accompaniment that the phalanxes and columns of troops paraded down the Champs Elysées on 14 July 1939 in the customary review to mark the country's national day. It was an unusually spectacular occasion. As one observer put it, 'Never had the French Army looked more magnificent.' Past the reviewing stands tramped those regiments whose own histories had imparted such resplendence to their country's: the steel-helmeted infantry, led by officers with drawn swords; Chasseurs; Zouaves; Marines; Foreign Legionaries; cavalry, including the splendid North African Spahis in their flowing cloaks. There were, too, the representatives of the new kinds of warfare: the squadrons of clanking and rumbling tanks, turret-hatches open, their commanders coming smartly to the 'eyes right' as they saluted the President of the Republic and the leaders of its armed forces. Meanwhile overhead zoomed, in chevron after chevron, the winged might of the Air Force.

Among the guests of honor invited to witness the scene was the British Minister of War, Leslie Hore-Belisha, and at his side a Parliamentary colleague not un-

known to his hosts, Winston Churchill. Aware, as by this time even the most blindly optimistic were, that a terrible and ever-growing cloud overshadowed the European sky, his pugnacious, baby-face beamed, we are told, as he watched this show of strength by his country's closest ally and neighbor.

'Thank God for the French Army,' he said.

It was a cry of relief from the heart. He had long urged his country to prepare itself against what at first only he and a pitiful few like him had seen coming, and he knew how little and how late his pleas had been heeded.

This reluctance to arm was not difficult to understand. The legacy of World War I, with its endless casualty lists and the horrors of the trenches, was a deeply ingrained loathing of war and everything associated with it. In that climate, as John Kennedy wrote, 'Armaments were looked upon as something horrible, as being the causes of war, not a means of defense.' It was not guns the British people wanted. It was not even butter. For many, for the million and a half unemployed, for example, it was bread. To squander money on instruments of death was, in these circumstances, little short of immoral.

The forces were pared down to the bone and any suggestion they should be increased or re-equipped bitterly resented.

The Royal Navy, ever the first line of

defense was, it is true, still formidable, even if less so than formerly. It was, however, vulnerable to the submarine and mine as well as to attack from the skies where, as most people predicted, much of a future war would be waged.

The Royal Air Force, whose task it was to defend those skies, possessed two splendid fighters in the *Hurricane* and *Spitfire*, but their numbers were grossly deficient. And where were the long-range bombers? Most important, where were the dive bombers?

The Army was in good heart, though kept down to the size needed to police the Empire and organized mainly for this purpose. It would be increased by the National Service Act passed in April 1939. It would take time, however, to equip and train the new recruits.

As for its commanders, gallant and conscientious as they were, they were as hostile to new ideas and as lacking in imagination as in Crimean times. In Germany the worst abuse that could be hurled at a war plan was to say it had been created by the British General Staff!

'Thank God,' Churchill could say fervently, 'for the French Army.'

It was not only numerically strong, but it seemed to be adequately supplied

Below: Foreign Minister von Ribbentrop, Prime Minister Chamberlain and Hitler at Munich in September 1938.

with the most up-to-date weapons. It was, for example, particularly strong in firepower with some ninety guns per division, as well as antitank and anti-aircraft guns, making a total of 11,000 in all. Along its Northeast Front which ran from Basel to the sea, it could dispose no fewer than ninety-four divisions. Seventy of these were infantry, three were armored, while the remainder were light mechanized, cavalry and fortress divisions. There was in addition ex-Sergeant Major André Maginot's engineering master-piece, the line of fortifications which bore his name and which faced France's traditional enemy, Germany.

It was undoubtedly impressive and General Maxime Weygand, second-in-command to the great Foch in 1918 when he dragged victory out of defeat, felt able to tell an audience in Lille ten days before the Champs Elysées' parade, 'I believe that the French Army is a more effective force than at any time in its history. Its materiel is first-rate, its fortifications first class, its morale is excellent, its high command remarkable.' He should have been in a position to know. He had been Commander in Chief from 1931 to 1935.

But did he? Not all thought so. About half the guns making up its vaunted firepower were the 75-mms of the 1914–18 War, effective then but out-matched by the larger calibers of other armies. For its movement the infantry would still have to rely on its feet because

Hitler in Prague after its seizure in March 1939.

of a shortage of trucks. Only one division in every nine was mechanized. The Air Force, by no means small, was equipped with aircraft whose performance was doubtful. The tanks were well armored and powerful, but there were too few of the best models. The whole plan for rearmament was held up by strikes and bureaucracy. Aircraft production averaged 37 a month against Germany's 1000 a month.

French Premier Daladier bows to Mussolini at Munich.

Over the soldier himself, the *poilu*, in his thick khaki uniform, many imponderables hung. The Army had suffered atrociously in World War I, its 1,500,000 casualties cutting a wide swathe out of France's comparatively small population. In 1917

Below: Hitler, Mussolini, Ciano, von Ribbentrop and Daladier at the Munich Conference.

Left: Der Führer and Il Duce on a Roman balcony in 1939 after they formed the Pact of Steel.

the Army had mutinied against what it saw as useless carnage and there were few who could be sure no similar revolt would take place if it was to be threatened with the recurrence of experiences like the Battle of Verdun. As for the nation itself, from which the *poilu* came, this had been shaken by a succession of governmental crises and scandals and in 1936 by something approaching civil war. The peasantry which formed the bulk of the population in an agrarian country would almost certainly regard enemy occupation as preferable to destruction of standing crops, farmstead and village they had experienced a quarter of a century before. The middle and intellectual classes were divided between those who supported the Popular Front of left-wing parties and those who saw the Front as an outpost of Moscow, whose sole opponents were Hitler and Mussolini.

The High Command continued to proclaim itself the successor of Napoleon and hence the fount of all military wisdom, and was as hidebound by dogma as it had been in 1914. Then the prevailing doctrine had been *l'offensive à l'outrance*, offensive to the utmost, in whose cause countless numbers had been sent to die on the German barbed wire with the chatter of machine guns in their ears. Now the pendulum had swung its full distance; defense was paramount and with it the theoretically impervious continuous line.

There were, of course, those who warned against this complacency, who dared to suggest that new weapons had reinstated the war of movement over the war of attrition. One such was a young tank corps commander, Charles de Gaulle. Even the hero of Verdun, Marshal of France, Philippe Pétain, made such a declaration as early as 1935.

Weygand's 'first class' fortifications consisted of La Ligne Maginot, of course. Startling as its achievement was, it still covered only 150 kilometers of France's 800 kilometers of frontier. It ended abruptly some distance from the Belgian border, at Montmédy, leaving an area exposed which Clausewitz called 'the pit of the French stomach.' For their part, the General Staff decided that the area lying to the east of the gap, and consisting largely of forest, was impenetrable, though earlier they had forecast an attack from this direction.

What concerned the more radical military minds, however, was the size of the forces the line was tying down. No

Left: Generals Keitel, von Stülpnagel and von Blaskowitz tell Hitler how they will occupy the Sudetenland prior to the Munich Conference.

fewer than one division in seven on the Northeast Front was involved in garrisoning it. Furthermore life within its confines affected the fighting mentality. Its denizens were less soldiers than troglodytes — which is what the satirical papers called them — quite unsuited to positional warfare should they be faced with it.

In 1939 Alan Brooke, later to be Britain's Chief of the Imperial General Staff, wrote in his diary of the complacency it bred and of the shattering blow to French morale in general which would come from its failure.

In addition to all these considerations, there was between the two allies, Britain and France, a deep suspicion, not to mention hostility. The French had not forgotten that in 1904 Britain had refused to commit herself to a treaty of friendship and mutual defense, only to an *entente*

And before that British foreign policy had been consistently anti-French and pro-German. To be sure, Britain and France had fought *bras-sous-bras* from 1914 to 1918, but that coalition had frequently been an uneasy one with recriminations by both.

Now there was on the one side the fear that Britain would commit France to an unpopular war and then fail to pull her weight, on the other a concern that the French might falter, leaving a British Expeditionary Force stranded.

Across the French frontier, within reach of the guns of the Maginot Line, a totally different picture presented itself. The National Socialist government of Adolf Hitler had seized power in January 1933 and quickly converted the nation into a vast armed camp, mobilizing all ages and

both sexes. Dynamic, aggressive and questing, it was also to French alarm, openly *revanchiste*, that is to say, seeking requittal for the blow to German military honor (as most Germans saw it) inflicted in 1918 and the humiliations which followed it. In particular there was the rankling memory of the French occupation of the Ruhr in 1921 and 1923 and its attendant brutalities. Should the Germans ever set out on the path of revenge, they possessed a sharp and well-honed instrument for the purpose: a military machine rebuilt, refurbished and retuned.

That this was so was certainly not because its General Staff was more imaginative or pragmatic than its French or British opposite numbers. It was the result of circumstances. The dictated Versailles peace treaty of June 1919 had been intended to ensure that Germany

The Munich Pact

Hitler's seizure of the Sudetenland left Germany free to decide the fate of Eastern Europe with the collaboration of the Soviet Union.
Below: Prime Minister Neville Chamberlain waves the Munich Agreement.
Left: Hitler and Martin Bormann (left) in Danzig after its seizure on the first day of World War II.
Inset below: Greater Germany just before the outbreak of World War II.

August 1939

German expansion in Europe

could never again rise up as a military threat. Not only were her armed forces to be restricted to 100,000 men, but she was to be limited in the number and size of tanks, aircraft and battleships. Thus, while in France and Britain striking power was equated with size, Germany had to shape a diametrically opposed military philosophy.

What emerged was largely the work of a group of army intellectuals who coalesced around General Hans von Seeckt, Commander in Chief of the Reichswehr from 1920 to 1926. For all his ramrod back and monocle, he was by no means the blood and iron reactionary of Prussian militarism in whom the iron predominated from uniform collar up (he

believed, for example, that the army should occupy the same neutral position in Germany that it did in the democracies). He had already proved his ability on the Russian Front in 1915 when his planning made possible the great Austro-German breakthrough which finally led to the defeat of the Tsar's armies and to his own subsequent downfall.

Seeckt and his group had imbibed the ideas of the British tank expert, Major General John Fuller, and of the military historian, Basil Liddell Hart, a ruthless critic of the Allied command in World War I and the exponent of the 'rushing torrent' theory of attack. According to this theory the aim of the assaulting forces was not to push the enemy back along

wide frontages, as was so often attempted between 1914 and 1918, but to smash a breach and then push through it with maximum speed, widening the gap in the process, as water will when it breaks through a sea wall. The objective, as he repeatedly declared, was not to break into the enemy lines, but through them, to reach its rear and communications.

The way to achieve this lay not in bigger, less mobile and, of necessity, fewer weapons, but in large numbers of small, faster-moving ones always used in close combination. It also involved employing all the elements simultaneously. The enemy front was first softened with artillery bombardment, then air attacks would strike deep into its rear, while the

armor, first making its own gap, fanned in either direction to envelop the defense from behind. Only then would the infantry come in to complete the destruction and seize the enemy's strongpoints.

It was a bold new concept — so new and so bold indeed that many shied away from it. However, under an arrangement with Soviet Russia, Seeckt was able to employ his tiny forces as a kind of military test-bench in exercises held in Kazan where they were far from prying eyes. The results showed the practicability of the idea, though the details needed to be refined.

When Seeckt was sacked by a jealous Hindenburg who became President of the German Republic in 1925, the torch

he lit was carried on by a thirty-eight-year-old staff Major, Heinz Guderian. He, too, knew his Fuller and his Liddell Hart. But he took them a stage further, developing a completely revolutionary notion — the tank division. No more was armor to be a mere adjunct to infantry; it was to be used as once cavalry had been, in overwhelming numbers, swarming among the defenders. For this purpose a 'breakthrough' tank had to be developed — fast, hard-hitting and with the longest attainable cruising range.

By 1935, thanks largely to Hitler's conversion to his ideas, the first three tank divisions were formed and Guderian, still only a colonel, was given command of one of them. His promotion thereafter was rapid: a lieutenant general early in 1938, he ended the year as a full general when he was appointed Chief of the Mobile Troops of the General Staff. The word *Blitzkrieg* had yet to be coined, but one element of it, the *Panzer*, had been born.

Left: Hitler and Mussolini in Munich, followed by Hermann Göring and Count Ciano on 29 September 1938.
Below: Luftwaffe Generals Milch and Christiansen before the outbreak of war.

So had another. Ernst Udet, a former member of Richthofen's 'Flying Circus' of World War I aces, was second only to the 'Red Baron' in the number of kills (sixty-two to his eighty). After the war he eked out a living as a film stunt flyer and by giving displays of aerobatics. In 1936 Hermann Göring, who had commanded the Richthofen Squadron after the baron's death, offered him a post in his own Air Ministry. During a visit to America soon after, he saw and flew a Curtiss *Hawk* being used, *inter alia*, as a dive bomber and was won over to the idea of this as a means of attack, a form, one might say, of mobile artillery.

The outcome was the Junkers-87 *Sturzkampfflugzeug* (or dive-attack aircraft), the name later being abbreviated to 'Stuka.' It was the last of a line of largely experimental dive bombers and the only one showing any promise.

By 1936, the two major weapons ready, the chance to use them in actual combat conditions occurred when, in July, the Spanish Civil War broke out and the Germans and Italians threw their weight on the side of the Nationalists under Francisco Franco. His ultimate victory owed much to the use of these new weapons, employed in close combination.

DROLE D[

Wehrmacht troops at the North
Cape in Norway after its occupation.

GUERRE

BLITZKRIEG
1940

Britain, France,
Belgium, Holland
and Germany,
1 September 1939
– 9 May 1940

But an even greater chance came three years later — on 1 September 1939, with the invasion of Poland. The Polish Army was by no means insignificant. Its peacetime strength of 370,000 could be expanded to 2,800,000 by the mobilization of its reservists. It was well trained and disciplined. While it was true that it had only one tank brigade, it believed the deficiency was more than made up for by its eleven cavalry brigades. These had played a crucial role in the victorious struggle against the Russian Bolsheviks from 1919 to 1920, when, by one of history's ironies, they were commanded by Maxime Weygand. (It was his revulsion at Bolshevik atrocities then which was said to have given him his undying hatred of anything connected with the Left.)

Before the German onslaught now, however, the suicidal bravery of the cavalry and infantry was only empty heroism. It was on the plains of Poland that the name *Blitzkrieg* gained currency, for using the new tactics, Pomerania and Silesia and the cities of Poznan, Cracow and Gdynia fell before what were very like strokes of lightning. By 12 September almost the whole of western Poland was in German hands.

Britain and France, which had gone to war on Poland's behalf, watched paralyzed. It is tempting to excuse this (as it was at the time) on the grounds of the difficulty of getting help to a small nation separated from its allies by the land mass of the German Reich, particularly in view of the speed of events. But as was shown

later, paralysis of the will was the principal characteristic of Franco-British command. At the outbreak of war this had been placed in the hands of Maurice Gamelin. Now sixty-seven, he had been a staff officer in World War I, when his self-effacing demeanor had served him well. He acquired a masklike expression some described as inscrutable and others as the blankness of stupidity. He soon earned himself the sobriquet 'Gaga-melin.'

His overriding concern at this stage was to see that the war did not open with a Verdun of his making, and when someone suggested that an attack of some kind might be in order, he answered

Above: Hitler, followed by Bormann, is saluted by SS-Gruppenführer Wolff on the Polish Front in September 1939.
Right: A squadron of Ju-87 Stukas over Poland.

angrily that he did not 'intend to break his best troops in the first battle.' Thus his sole response in honor of a prewar pledge given to Poland to attack 'within fifteen days of mobilization' was to move a token force in the Saar up to an advanced line

Below: Prewar tanks are mobilized for the Polish campaign.

of outposts. The enemy took it in the best possible spirit: their electricity generating stations continued to provide power for several villages on the French side.

Otherwise the French did nothing in particular. There were scarcely any German troops there, because they were needed in Poland. Had the assault been vigorous, the way to the heart of Germany would have been found open.

The fall of Poland was followed first by the removal of the French – and some British – troops from their advanced outposts in the Saar and then the informal truce of what came to be called in Britain the 'Phony War' and in France the '*drôle de guerre*.'

Below: Hitler and his generals survey the action near Warsaw in September 1939. From right to left: Generals von Reichenau, Paulus (obscured), Rommel, Hitler, Keitel and Bormann.
Right: French General Gamelin views a map of the Western Front during the 'Phony War.' Britain and France stood aside as Germany conquered Poland.
Far right: Hitler salutes his troops as they closed in on Warsaw, 21 September 1939.

Within forty-eight hours of the declaration of war, units of the British Expeditionary Force, as the nation's continental army was called, began crossing the Channel, though as their allies were consistently to complain, in numbers far too small. They had been put under the command of General Viscount Gort, a charming, burly former Guards' officer, scion of one of those Anglo-Irish families which had provided so many British soldiers. Affable, far from unintelligent and in many ways a modernist (he was one of the first British officers to learn how to fly his own plane), he suffered in the eyes of his contemporaries from a preoccupation with the minutiae of army life rather than with the broad sweeps of strategy. However, the BEF did take three men to France who were later to acquire some renown. One was Major General Bernard Montgomery, commanding its 3rd Division; the second was Lieutenant General Alan Brooke, commanding its II Corps; the third, Major General Harold Alexander, 1st Division commander.

Administratively the BEF came under French command with the right of appeal to its own government. In practical terms this meant it was part of the long North-east Front from Switzerland to the sea, whose commander, General Georges, was, after January 1940, interposed between Gamelin (who could not stand him) and the armies in the line.

Whatever Gort's shortcomings, he at least found useful activity for his growing forces in both improving its combat-readiness and in building a defensive line along its allotted sector which ran down part of the Franco-Belgian border. Later the Germans were to speak of the British troops as their only serious opponents.

By contrast, such was their faith in the invincibility of the Maginot Line, that the entire period from the fall of Poland became one of inactivity for the French Army, boredom and quite literally of 'French leave.' The effects on morale were predictable enough. One manifestation of it was drunkenness on such a scale that special 'sobering-up' rooms had to be installed at the railway stations.

Morale was further undermined by the ceaseless propaganda barrage from the German side, aimed principally at driving

a wedge of suspicion between the two members of the wartime coalition by trying to show that the British were going to allow the French to sacrifice themselves in a war of imperial aggrandizement. This was reinforced with threats of a blow shortly to fall which, compared to all that occurred in the last war, would seem like a picnic. These efforts were especially effective in an army which had little faith in its own General Staff or the nation's leaders and which dreaded the war in any case.

That the Maginot Line was as invincible as it was claimed to be was a contention no one cared to try. On the contrary, the Germans, somewhat belatedly, had reacted by building their own version of it, the Siegfried Line. By the outbreak of war this was far from completion (and never was completed), but by showing off selected parts of it to neutral press men it was possible to convey the idea it was at least the equal of the French showpiece.

The position along the two fortified lines being one of deadlock, the only way the belligerents could get to grips with one another was via Switzerland or Belgium and, possibly, the Netherlands. For the Allies this would necessitate the morally unthinkable course of violating the neutrality of these countries. The Allies realized that the Germans might feel less delicacy in this, but asked, why increase the numbers against them?

At the root, this opposition of irresistible force and immovable object was not altogether distasteful. Time was on the Allies' side, it was said. They were growing in strength every month, why should they hurry? But there was besides a tiny spark of hope aglimmer in many French and some British breasts as well. Honor had been satisfied with the declaration of war on Poland's behalf. Perhaps now there was a slim chance that some benevolent neutral might come along with a peace formula. Good sense would prevail, and everyone would go home.

The French had openly declared that they did not regard Poland as worth a single soldier's life. Thirty-six hours after the German invasion, when the Polish ambassador in Paris pressed for the fulfillment of the treaty obligation to attack, he was told by the Minister of Foreign Affairs, 'You don't expect us to have a massacre of women and children in Paris, do you?' In other words, the enemy must not be provoked. The British view was scarcely different. When it was suggested that the Black Forest, where there were large arms' caches, should be set ablaze with incendiary raids, the Air Minister gave the Alice-in-Wonderland answer, 'Are you aware it is private property?'

No one was anxious to fire the first shot in Germany's direction. However, the possibility of an attack coming via Holland or Belgium had not been overlooked. Pre-war approaches had been made to both

to allow an extension of the Maginot Line across their frontiers with Germany but both countries had refused. Bitter as the French were at this, there is little doubt that the decision was prudent. The line had been under construction since 1929, its progress being marked by the fits and starts of the French economy, and it was never completely finished. Had the Dutch and Belgians allowed its extension and had further crises caused postponement, they would have found themselves with something infinitely worse than useless: a fortified line whose establishment would have increased German antagonism, but which could do little to save them from German wrath.

Besides, the Belgians had suffered even more than the French in the last war. Almost the entire country had been under harshly repressive occupation from the first months of the war. The recollection

Above: A squadron of Heinkel He-111 bombers over Poland.

of those years was still fresh in the national memory. Since nothing it did could render so small a country invulnerable, its only chance lay in avoiding war altogether. To this end, the king, Leopold III, had in 1936 revoked the mutual defense treaty between his own country, France and Britain. Not even informal inter-staff meetings were permitted thereafter and this state of affairs continued after the outbreak of hostilities.

For their part, the Dutch preferred to rely on a tradition of non-involvement in the affairs of their bigger neighbors and on their long-standing friendship with Germany. It was to Holland that Kaiser Wilhelm II had fled after his abdication in 1918; in the twenties when the German people had suffered so atrociously under

22

October 1939

German expansion in Europe

the postwar depression and their own inflation, it was the Dutch more than anyone else who had rushed to their aid, opening their borders so that hungry German children could eat at Dutch tables. These children would now have grown into the soldiers of the Third Reich. Was it possible that they could turn to bite the feeding hand? Besides, of what conceivable strategic value was Holland, so far from the main cockpit of the struggle? Both countries had, in any case, internal problems sufficient to force them to hesitate before entering a war against Germany. Belgium had the problem of its Dutch-speaking Flemish minority, seeking separation from the French-speaking majority of the country and whose growing militancy had been encouraged by Germany from as early as World War I. There was also the extreme right-wing Royalist Party under Leon Degrelle which looked toward Germany and, especially toward Mussolini's Italy for inspiration. In Holland, where there had always been a section of public opinion which admired Germany, there was a group founded on

Below: A tank commander salutes Hitler during the Polish campaign.

Nazi lines which even had representation in the Dutch parliament.

For all this, there had been an increased awareness of the threat from the east during the middle to late thirties. Its consequence was a repairing of the fences in that direction. In 1936 the Belgians had increased the period of military service and had modernized their fortifications. The positions between Liège and Namur, scene of the early fighting in August 1914, were reinforced and a new line established along the Albert canals from Maastricht to Antwerp. By 1939 the Belgian Army numbered twenty-three divisions of infantry, plus two of cavalry and two of Chasseurs Ardennais (a frontier guard unit) which was partially motorized, making 600,000 men in all. There was, however, no armor and no more than a token Air Force of out-of-date machines.

These measures on the part of their neighbor left the Dutch feeling especially exposed. The length of their frontier with Germany made a fortress system economically impractical and the defense of the country was therefore based on a two-point plan: the inundation of the low-lying land to make it impassable and the withdrawal of the defenders to what was

Above left: Germany's four-pronged attack against Poland in September 1939.
Above center: The partition of Poland at the end of September.
Above: Greater Germany after the Polish conquest.

called 'Fortress Holland,' a rough triangle which included Amsterdam, The Hague and Rotterdam. The Army, comprising eleven divisions almost entirely of infantry, would endeavor to hold this until help reached them by sea. To give time for concentration, an advanced line, the Grebbe, which ran southward from the Ijsselmeer to the Neder Rijn and to the region of the Peel marshes, would be used to impede the enemy's advance.

If the Dutch and Belgians could be accused of complacency in the face of reality, there is no doubt that this was repeatedly shaken. Almost from the war's outbreak there was a flow of protests from Germany accusing both Holland and Belgium of failing to be impartial.

Often protest was accompanied by threat and there was a series of alarms, the most serious of which occurred on 12 November 1939. (It was later found that this was the original date set by Hitler for the invasion.) Another came on 10 January 1940 when a Messerschmitt 108 made a forced landing near Mechelen just inside the Belgian border. Its passenger, a German staff officer, Hellmuth Reinberger, was captured before he could destroy the contents of his briefcase, the plans for an attack on France along precisely the route which the French and British General Staffs had predicted. The public reaction verged on panic. General Vandenbergen, the Belgian Chief of Staff, on his own initiative removed the barricades between his country and France, and opened immediate talks on mutual defense with his French opposite number.

Above right: German soldiers in front of propaganda banners on the Rhine which ask French troops why they are at war.
Right: Wehrmacht troops on the Siegfried Line in 1939.

The Phony War

Throughout the winter of 1939–40 German and French soldiers bombarded each other with propaganda loudspeakers and placards.
Far right: German Army magazine advertises the West Wall tank traps.
Right: The Franco-German border at Oberrhein. The banner reads: Hitler says I have never wavered in my desire to bury the ancient enmity between Germany and France.
Below: A patriotic French poster along the West Wall at Oberrhein.
Bottom: Another banner reads: Hitler says after 15 days of bombardment the war propagandists would quickly change their view.
Bottom right Construction of the Siegfried Line continued during the 'Phony War.'

DIE WEHRMACHT

AUSGABE A

Berlin, 17. Mai 1944
8. Jahrgang Nr. 1
Belgien 3,15 Fr., Bulg. 8 L.
Dänemark 40 Øre, Finnland
4,50 mk., Frankreich 4 Fr.,
Ital. 2 L., Kroatien 15 Kuna
Niederl. 20 Cts., Norwegen
40 Øre, Portugal 2,— Esc.,
Rumän. 20 Lei, Serb. 5 Dinar,
Spanien 1,25 Pts., Schweden
45 Öre, Schweiz 45 Rappen,
Slowakei 2,50 Ks., Türkei
12.50 Kurus, Ungarn 46 fillér

HERAUSGEGEBEN VOM OBERKOMMANDO DER WEHRMACHT

When the attack failed to materialize, it was assumed that the whole thing was a German deception. The Brussels' government ordered the re-establishment of the barricades and the breaking off of the inter-staff talks, though they continued in secret. The harsh fact was that small nations had had the daunting experience of seeing what had been allowed to happen to Poland. If this hardly helped confidence, there was also a lingering doubt about the state of French morale.

Below: Grenade-throwing is taught by a British officer in France in early 1940.

Yet a species of Franco-Belgian defense plan did emerge from the secret talks. The River Dyle, with its estuary on Antwerp, follows a southerly course past Mechelen (Malines), Louvain and Wavre to reach its source at Genappe. The Allied line of the 'Dyle Plan' would follow the river to Wavre, then continue this southward tendency along the Meuse through Namur and Dinant before crossing the French border, going down to Mézières, then, still along the northern bank of the Meuse, down to Sedan to cross the river at Montmédy where it would join up with the shoulder of the Maginot Line. It was shorter than the straggling Belgian frontier

Above: A British motorcycle team of the BEF are greeted by French villagers near the Belgian frontier.

with Germany and so more easily defended, but it had two great demerits. It virtually cut Belgium in half and therefore meant the abandonment of the area east of the Dyle. It also meant that British and French forces, who were to join the Belgians in manning it, would have to unseat themselves from the strong defense lines they had been preparing since the outbreak of war and pivot on Montmédy to take up their new ones. What was more they would be doing this only after an invasion had begun, since the Belgians refused to countenance the plan being carried out before. These factors alone should have led to its rejection.

Far from this happening, the various units involved were assigned the places they would take up and to give them a chance to do so, the Belgian Army was to hold its fortified line along the Albert Canal which was thought unlikely to fall in less than five days. The key to this was the fortress of Eben Emael, covering the city and road junction of Liège and its approach roads as well as the canal itself. The fort was of modern design with interlocking fields of fire and incorporated all the latest knowledge of fortification in which the Belgians were regarded as pre-eminent. There was a general conviction that the enemy would find it a hard nut to crack, though the Belgians also realized that, if it fell, it would allow the enemy to use the road system round Liège and Maastricht to pour into the country with Antwerp and Brussels open to attack.

The apprehensions which the small nations like Holland and Belgium felt were hardly alleviated by the events of the spring of 1940. For the German war effort, one indispensable need was high quality steel from Sweden. Its access route lay via the North Sea, easily

Below: Anti-gassing equipment and clothing are tested by a group of British officers in France.
Bottom: Generals Axmann and Falkenhorst sit next to the Norwegian traitor Vidkun Quisling after the seizure of Oslo.

blockaded by the Royal Navy. To ensure a land route, therefore, Hitler invaded Denmark and Norway on 9 April. The Danes gave in within twenty-four hours; indeed they did not attempt to resist. In Norway, however, there was a struggle and the British and French rushed such aid as they could to it. It was late in arriving and in any case pitifully inadequate. The struggle dragged on to mid-May, with the Allies holding the port of Narvik until forced to evacuate, because the men were needed elsewhere.

As far as Holland and Belgium were concerned this period was marked by an increase in German friendliness toward them, with Hitler giving assurances about their territorial integrity.

It was the mark of the Nazis' duplicity that these pledges were being offered while they were actively planning to overrun their recipients. The Dutch might question the strategic value of their country to the war, but Hitler was thinking

beyond the immediate task of reaching the enemy in France. He had in mind that Britain might continue to resist from its island fortress once France had fallen and he needed well-equipped ports from which he could launch his invasion fleets.

The first German plan, drawn up by General Franz Halder and his staff, aimed at bringing all this about. Plan Yellow *(Fall Gelb)*, had been issued in October 1939, that is to say when the Polish campaign was just ending. It involved two Army Groups: Group A, consisting of two armies, under the overall command of Colonel General Gerd von Rundstedt, and Group B, under Colonel General Fedor von Bock, with three armies but also eight of the ten armored divisions available for the operation. The Germans did not spare their resources for some 137 divisions were earmarked for

Below: German troops disembark during the first landings in Norway.

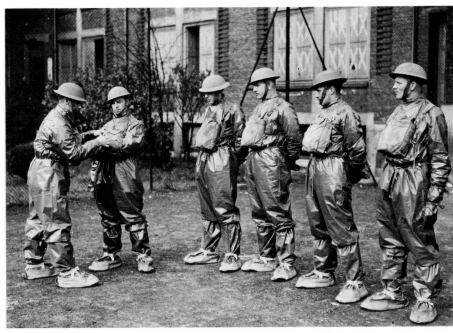

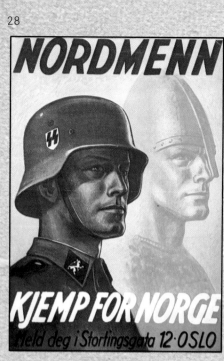

the campaign, seventy-four for the opening assault alone.

However, it was not numbers which were to make the difference but speed. The tactics of Blitzkrieg were once more to be used and for more surprise there would be no formal declaration of war. Tactically the plan envisaged the securing of a line Antwerp–Brussels–Namur, followed by a sweep to the sea in the area from Ostend southward. It aimed simply at separating the British and French forces from the Belgian and destroying them later. That was as far as it went. As Alistair Horne pointed out in *To Lose a Battle*, no one had considered how the

Far left: Nazi poster urges Norwegians to join the Waffen-SS. **Left:** Wehrmacht troops patrol a Norwegian street for snipers. **Right:** German transport is unloaded at a Norwegian port. **Below:** German troops greet the arrival of a supply ship.

final destruction of the enemy was to be accomplished. Manstein has gone so far as to say that it was suggested to him that the General Staff felt their chances of defeating France were 'slender, if not non-existent.'

It was this plan which had fallen into Allied hands in January. The revelation of their intentions was enough to stimulate redrafting, but besides it gave the critics a fresh chance. Among them was Erich von Manstein, then a lieutenant general and later Rundstedt's Chief of Staff, who for his pains had been sent to a remote command in eastern Germany. Now his ideas were resuscitated (though Hitler claimed them for his own), and the plan which resulted in February 1940 could be likened to two men holding another's arms while a third strikes a blow at the belly — indeed, that very 'stomach of France' Clausewitz had written of. Bock's Army Group B would seize the left or northern arm, which it was hoped would have reached out into Holland. And for this purpose, he had two Armies, the Eighteenth and Sixth, totalling twenty-eight divisions, and the support of Albert Kesselring's Second Air Fleet. The Eighteenth would include one Panzer Division to penetrate North Holland with airborne troops landing in 'Fortress Holland.' The Sixth, which included two Panzer and one motorized division, was to operate in Dutch Limburg and in Belgium north of the Meuse.

Left: Wreckage of Norwegian ships in a fjord after the German attack.
Right: Waffen-SS machine gunner takes aim in his bunker.

The enemy's right, or southern arm, which in this case was the shield-bearing one, since it contained the Maginot Line, was the responsibility of Army Group C under Field Marshal Wilhelm Ritter von Leeb. This was to hold the enemy on the Maginot Line and along the right bank of the Rhine up to Switzerland. It comprised a total of seventeen divisions in two Armies, the First and Seventh.

In the meantime von Rundstedt's Army Group A in conjunction with Hugo Sperrle's Third Air Force would attempt to breach the Allied line along the Meuse between Sedan and Namur and drive on to the sea at Abbeville, near the mouth of the Somme. The knuckles of this blow in the stomach would be supplied by a

Above: A Nazi battalion huddles behind a Pzkw-1 near Narvik where Norwegian opposition was fiercest.

Panzer group under General Ewald von Kleist. It would cross the Meuse between Dinant and Sedan, its right flank being covered by the Fourth Army, which was to advance along the Sambre-Meuse Valley, then link with Bock's Army Group B to envelop the enemy. The Twelfth Army would penetrate Belgium via Luxembourg following the armored forces, and the Sixteenth would enter Belgium also through south Luxembourg to protect the southern or left flank of the main attack. Two headquarters' Armies, the Ninth and Sixth, would then stand

guard over the Aisne, the canals and the Somme to ensure that the forces in the north could move freely.

Once the objective in Belgium had been achieved, the German forces would wheel left to envelop those south of the Somme and behind the Maginot Line. The plan, given the code name *Unternehmen Sichelschnitt* (Operation Scythestroke), was of a magnitude to take the breath away. What it was proposing was not simply to lay down the outlines for a single battle, even for a campaign. It was proposing to formulate in advance the shape of what was, in effect, an entire war. Manstein, quoting the Elder Moltke, reminded his readers that no plan could extend with certainty beyond the first encounter with the enemy. Thereafter it was only laymen who thought they could detect its outlines in subsequent events. That Moltke's caveat was so largely disproved in this case is an enormous tribute to the genius of the German General Staff.

Far left: A Dornier Do-17 bomber over the Norwegian coast.
Above left: Right propeller of a Junkers Ju-88 bomber.
Right: Wehrmacht troops parade through occupied Oslo.
Below: German troops near Narvik.

34

Above: Europe after the conquest of Denmark and Norway.

There remained, of course, the various details to be taken care of. Now that the main thrust was to fall to him, Rundstedt was given the additional strength of an entire new Army, plus seven of the ten Panzer divisions. This total sounds impressive only until one realizes that in numbers the French could fully match it. The Germans had some 2690 tanks with 800, mostly light, in reserve. The French had no fewer than 3000. They included the Hotchkiss-39 assault tank, the 20-ton Somua-25 with a 47-mm gun, and the ace in the French pack, the Char B, with

Below: German troops on the ships transporting them to Norwegian ports on 9 April.

both 75-mm and 45-mm guns and nearly double the thickness of armor of any of its rivals. Added to this were 384 British light tanks and 100 'infantry' tanks, including twenty-three new Matildas.

The German advantage lay not in numbers but in the difference in military attitude. Since, on the Allied side, infantry was still 'queen of the battlefield,' tanks were to be used for reconnaissance or screening purposes or to remove obstacles to its advance. Gamelin was on record as stating his belief that 'tanks could never achieve a breakthrough.' They would simply run out of gasoline. Inevitably this led to the dispersing of armor in small units, which were never available in the numbers required to counter the enemy's thrusts or to make thrusts of their own.

While furious planning and preparation were taking place on the German side, in the west there was calm which, if it could be described as unreal, was certainly not uneasy. The French General Staff continued to reiterate its parrot phrases about time being on their side. The enemy dared not attack and Allied strength was growing all the time. When asked to predict the moment of the great offensives, the new 'advances on Berlin,' the generals shrugged Gallic shoulders.

Against this background they went about the disposition of their forces and the leisurely strengthening of their lines, with occasional criticism of the British for their tardiness in arriving. Even by the spring of 1940 there were only ten

Above: The World War I Schlieffen Plan juxtaposed with the French and German plans of attack in 1940.

divisions of the BEF in the field and five of these were Territorials.

In fact the only real crises were governmental ones. The first came in March 1940 when Edouard Daladier, the French premier, and one of the signatories of the Munich Agreement of September 1938, was criticized for indecisiveness in the prosecution of the war and resigned to be succeeded by the far more energetic Paul Reynaud. A similar crisis in early

Above right: Wehrmacht troops poised for a further assault on Norwegian positions.
Right: The same squad attacks as their shelter-cover blazes.

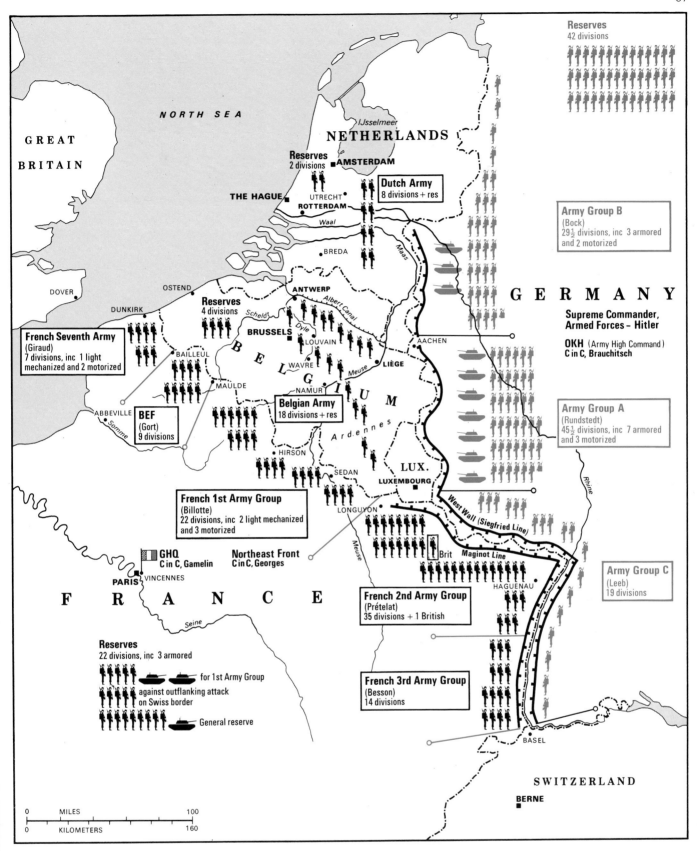

Reserves
42 divisions

NORTH SEA

GREAT BRITAIN

NETHERLANDS

Reserves
2 divisions ■ AMSTERDAM

Dutch Army
8 divisions + res

THE HAGUE ■
UTRECHT
ROTTERDAM

Waal

BREDA

Maas

Army Group B
(Bock)
29½ divisions, inc 3 armored
and 2 motorized

G E R M A N Y

**Supreme Commander,
Armed Forces – Hitler**

OKH (Army High Command)
C in C, Brauchitsch

DOVER

OSTEND

DUNKIRK

Reserves
4 divisions

ANTWERP

Albert Canal

Scheldt

Dyle

BRUSSELS ■
LOUVAIN

AACHEN

French Seventh Army
(Giraud)
7 divisions, inc 1 light
mechanized and 2 motorized

BAILLEUL

B E L
WAVRE
Meuse
LIÈGE

Army Group A
(Rundstedt)
45½ divisions, inc 7 armored
and 3 motorized

ABBEVILLE

Somme

MAULDE

NAMUR

G
I
U
M

BEF
(Gort)
9 divisions

Belgian Army
18 divisions + res

Ardennes

HIRSON

LUX.
LUXEMBOURG

West Wall (Siegfried Line)

SEDAN

French 1st Army Group
(Billotte)
22 divisions, inc 2 light mechanized
and 3 motorized

LONGUYON

Meuse

Brit
Maginot Line

Rhine

GHQ
C in C, Gamelin

Northeast Front
C in C, Georges

Army Group C
(Leeb)
19 divisions

PARIS ■ VINCENNES

HAGUENAU

Seine

F R A N C E

French 2nd Army Group
(Prételat)
35 divisions + 1 British

Reserves
22 divisions, inc 3 armored

for 1st Army Group

against outflanking attack
on Swiss border

General reserve

French 3rd Army Group
(Besson)
14 divisions

BASEL

S W I T Z E R L A N D

■ **BERNE**

```
0        MILES          100
0      KILOMETERS       160
```

**Above far left: German soldiers patrol the Norwegian countryside as their occupation continued.
Above left: Danish King Christian rides alone through Copenhagen's streets as he did each morning of the occupation.
Far left: Canadian and New Zealand POWs box.
Left: Ju-52 transport coasts over Arctic waters near the Norwegian coast viewed from the AA position on a German ship offshore.**

May 1940 almost brought a pre-emptory end to Reynaud's career and, with it, that of Gamelin, but this was averted.

The British premier, Neville Chamberlain, the main architect of Munich, who had been dubbed by the French *Monsieur J'aime Berlin*, was less fortunate. An acrimonious debate in the House of Commons began on 7 May with many Conservative members siding with the Labour Opposition in a vote of censure on the government's conduct of the war, particularly with reference to the fiasco of

Above: Relative strengths of the Western Allies and the Third Reich on the eve of the Blitzkrieg. The numerical strength of the Dutch, Belgian, French and British armies exceeded German manpower.

Norway. The upshot was his resignation and succession by Winston Churchill as head of a National Government of all parties. This change in midstream was one which more than anything else helped to change the tide of war.

THE FALL OF T

HE FORTRESS

The center of Rotterdam after its destruction by the Luftwaffe on 14 May 1940.

The Commons' debaters were still in the full flood of oratory as the first blows fell. On 8 May Viscount Davignon, Belgian Ambassador in Berlin, warned that a German ultimatum to his government was being prepared. When the Dutch discovered they were to be the recipients of a similar document, they realized, for the first time, that Germany's National Socialists were not to be restrained by feelings of friendship or of gratitude toward their neighbors. Hitler's plans demanded the Dutch ports. That was all. Leave in both the Dutch and Belgian armed forces was cancelled. On 9 May, however, the Belgian Chief of Staff, apparently believing this was yet another false alarm, allowed his men leave.

At 2300 that night National Socialists in the Grand Duchy of Luxembourg received word that German troops were soon to pass through and the Socialists were urged to ensure their safe and unresisted passage.

Although warned of this, the Brussels' government remained adamant that the national territory had to be violated before French aid was sought. They had not long to wait. As the night wore on troop movements across the border could actually be heard and in the early hours of the morning there were reports of German aircraft flying over Belgium. At 0430 came first news of frontier crossings. Less than an hour later the first air raid on Brussels' airport began. But it was at 0505 on that morning of Friday, 10 May that reports came in which showed how totally irrelevant all the preparations to hold back the flood had been.

The German High Command had been as clear as anyone else about the commanding importance of the Belgian defense line and in particular the fort of Eben Emael. The plan for its speedy capture was as radical and daring as anything evolved by either side thereafter. Frontal attacks would have been extremely costly and would have put a brake on an operation whose success depended on speed and consequent surprise. The solution adopted and here used for the first time was a gliderborne assault; the task force selected was the Koch Storm Detachment, formed under Captain Koch at Hildesheim in November 1939, six months before the attack came. Preparation was carried out in such secrecy that leave was forbidden to the participating units which, including paratroops and sappers, numbered only eighty-five in all.

Eleven gliders were to land on the fort itself and the seven or eight men in each were to take two emplacements. At the same time, other units were to advance from the frontier to take the bridges across the canal on either side of Eben Emael and so allow the waiting Panzers to advance.

Right: Dutch civilians watch as the city center of Rotterdam burns.
Far right: The German attack on the Low Countries.
Below: Dutch ship of the Holland-America Line burns in Rotterdam harbor after aerial assault.
Below right: Dutch soldiers load their 10cm artillery.

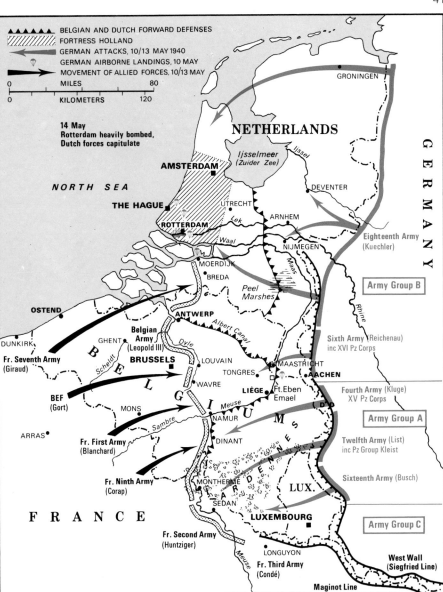

BELGIAN AND DUTCH FORWARD DEFENSES
FORTRESS HOLLAND
GERMAN ATTACKS, 10/13 MAY 1940
GERMAN AIRBORNE LANDINGS, 10 MAY
MOVEMENT OF ALLIED FORCES, 10/13 MAY

MILES 80
KILOMETERS 120

14 May
Rotterdam heavily bombed,
Dutch forces capitulate

NETHERLANDS

GERMANY

Ijsselmeer
(Zuider Zee)

NORTH SEA

AMSTERDAM

Ijssel

DEVENTER

THE HAGUE

UTRECHT

ARNHEM

ROTTERDAM

Lek

Eighteenth Army
(Kuechler)

Waal

NIJMEGEN

MOERDIJK

Maas

Army Group B

BREDA

Peel
Marshes

Rhine

OSTEND

ANTWERP

Albert Canal

Sixth Army (Reichenau)
inc XVI Pz Corps

DUNKIRK

GHENT

Belgian
Army
(Leopold III)

Dyle

BELGIUM

MAASTRICHT

Fr. Seventh Army
(Giraud)

BRUSSELS

LOUVAIN

TONGRES

AACHEN

Scheldt

WAVRE

LIÈGE

Ft. Eben
Emael

Fourth Army (Kluge)
XV Pz Corps

BEF
(Gort)

MONS

Meuse

NAMUR

Army Group A

Sambre

Fr. First Army
(Blanchard)

DINANT

Twelfth Army (List)
inc Pz Group Kleist

ARRAS

Fr. Ninth Army
(Corap)

ARDENNES

MONTHERME

Sixteenth Army (Busch)

LUX.

SEDAN

FRANCE

LUXEMBOURG

Army Group C

Fr. Second Army
(Huntziger)

Meuse

LONGUYON

Fr. Third Army
(Condé)

West Wall
(Siegfried Line)

Maginot Line

At 0430 on 10 May the gliders towed by Junkers-52 transports took off. Two got lost in the morning mist. One managed to reach its objective: the other, which failed to do so, was nonetheless able to add its men to the storm detachments detailed to take the bridges.

Landing on the fort took place without mishap. Although there was sporadic resistance, explosive charges in the gun emplacements successfully destroyed or disabled them. Further charges planted at the bottom of ascent shafts produced the maximum damage in the fort's confines and caused a large number of casualties. In the meantime the storm detachments, taking advantage of the fact that the enemy troops in Eben Emael were fully engaged, took the bridges and established bridgeheads with machine-gun units also dropped by parachute.

In a few hours Belgium's first line of defense, which it had been hoped could hold out for at least five days, was neutralized. This had been achieved by a means which no one on the Allied side expected would be used. One German

Left: Wehrmacht troops watch a ship leave Rotterdam.
Below: German anti-aircraftmen in The Hague shoot down remnants of the Dutch Air Force still in action.

participant in the assault recalls that there were no mines and little barbed wire to impede the gliders from landing. Preparations had been made for attacks from front or flanks; not for one coming from above. First news of the fall of Eben Emael reached Brussels as dawn broke. In its wake came the ululating of the air-raid sirens and the hum of aircraft, then the sound of explosions in the city itself.

It was decided to appeal to France and Britain immediately, but at this point it was found that the telephone was not working. At first sabotage or bomb damage was suspected, but it was discovered that the exchange operators, frightened at the bombing, had left their posts to go to the shelters. By 0730, with contact established, the Allied military missions entered Brussels.

Within hours the Anglo-French forces were moving in to take up their positions along the agreed line from Zeeland to Mézières. They had raced to the assistance of Dutch and Belgians, but had also done precisely what the German High Command had hoped. Liddell Hart was to

**Right: German troops begin the occupation of The Hague.
Below: German paratroops on the outskirts of Rotterdam after the first assault wave on 10 May.**

The remains of Rotterdam's city center after the rubble had been cleared. The heart of the city had been destroyed.

speak of a 'matador's cloak' waved by Bock's Army Group, tempting the Allies away from their strong defensive positions along the Franco-Belgian border. Hitler said he was ready to weep for joy at the news that this waving of the cloak had produced the desired effect. The British and French Armies had obligingly placed themselves in position for the planned envelopment.

But the truth is, whatever else, England and France had fulfilled their moral commitments. They had repeatedly appealed to Holland and Belgium to join them in providing a solid front to the enemy, but both countries had waited until five minutes past midnight before seeking aid.

Left: German soldiers disguised as Dutch police patrol a bridge across the Maas.
Below: German troops cross the Maas in South Holland.

Nazi Germany, which had repeatedly declared its intention of respecting Dutch and Belgian neutrality, had cynically and brutally invaded. The Allies had, even to their own disadvantage, respected it. When the call came, the Allies responded. Of course one cannot acquit them of self-interest or, for that matter, of blindness to reality. It was in their interest to keep Belgium fighting; they had failed to see the possibility of the blow which was to deprive them of their sword arm.

In passing judgment on the events and disasters of those mid-May and June days, it is important to keep the facts in mind and remember how they affected what came to pass later.

At 0830 that morning the German Ambassador presented himself to the

Right: Three German soldiers wave the white flag in Rotterdam after the bombing.

Above: Rotterdam in flames as the bombs fell on 14 May.

Above: Firefighters quenching the flames of the blazing city.

Belgian Foreign Minister, Paul-Henri Spaak, one of that country's and Europe's greatest statesmen. As he tried to take a paper from his pocket to hand to the minister, Spaak told him angrily, 'This is the second time in twenty-five years that Germany has committed a criminal aggression against a neutral and loyal Belgium.' As the Ambassador read his note which alleged that German action had been taken to forestall an invasion by Great Britain and France, Spaak took the document from him, in order, as he said, to spare him 'so painful a task.'

It was not only Belgium that was struck that Black Friday. At 0355 German planes began attacking the airport for Rotterdam at Waalhaven, as well as other

Below: Citizens evacuate their belongings from houses.

airports at Bergen, Schiphol and de Kooy, while The Hague itself was also under attack. As in the case of Belgium, word had gone out to France and Britain seeking their aid and in fact the French Seventh Army, under the command of the able General Henri Giraud, was making its way across the width of Belgium to form a junction with the Netherlands' forces in the Zeeland area.

But by 0500 hours airborne units from Kesselring's Second Air Fleet, part of Bock's Army Group, began dropping in and to the east of Waalhaven airfield. Although the Dutch forces fought with their customary courage they were unable to prevent its capture. In the meantime other airborne forces had been dropped north and south of the Moerdijk bridges near Dordrecht. Again, despite a determined defense, the Dutch were overpowered and unable to ensure even the destruction of the bridges.

Yet another airborne task force, this

time of only fifty men, landed at Feyenoord in south Rotterdam, which was separated from the main part of the city by the river, to capture the bridges across it. As they took up their positions some sixty seaplanes began landing on the river and debouching troops to hold the bridges. The area became the scene of heavy fighting with the Royal Netherlands' Marines, who earned themselves the title of the 'Black Devils' that day. An unsuccessful attempt was then made to retake the bridges with naval craft, while a destroyer of the Royal Netherlands' Navy sailed upstream for Rotterdam to try to prevent the German forces crossing northward into the city proper. Despite a heroic attempt to bring his ship as near as possible to Waalhaven airport and so within range of his guns, the captain was forced to withdraw or risk the loss of his

Preparations

Plans had long been laid for the combined attacks on the Low Countries and France. The first wave of troops would invade in the knowledge that the Netherlands would have been softened up by aerial attack and parachutists who would form an advance guard in the occupation of the heavily populated *Randstad*, the four principal cities of Amsterdam, Rotterdam, Utrecht and The Hague.

Below left: Stukas are loaded with bombs before the onslaught.

Bottom left: A consignment of bombs to be loaded on the Stukas.

Below right: Fighter crews get their final briefing from their commandant.

Bottom right: The dreaded dive bombers are loaded with aviation fuel.

vessel under the withering German air attack.

The airport remained in German hands and throughout the day some 250 Junkers-52s shuttled in an estimated 5000 men to reinforce the troops already there.

The purpose of these airborne attacks was, of course, to seal off Fortress Holland and to secure the routes by which the main German forces could advance toward it. These were already on the move, and by the evening of 10 May elements of the Eighteenth Army had crossed the Dutch-German border and entered Deventer, Arnhem and Nijmegen. They had even managed to take intact one bridge across the Maas and to pierce the extreme left of the Dutch line where it reached down toward Belgium.

Coincidentally with the other airborne assaults, paratroops began dropping on The Hague at 0500 with the purpose of occupying the Dutch capital and capturing its government. The airfields of Ockenburg, Ypenburg and Valkenburg were taken, though the first two only after bitter fighting. At Ypenburg, in particular, eleven of the thirteen air transports bringing up the German troops were destroyed. In fact the first waves of the attackers were mopped up, despite some internal resistance by Dutch Nazis, secretly armed, who actually fought against their own armed forces. However, the resistance in The Hague not only

**Below: A deserted street in Rotterdam as the bombs fell.
Below right: Rotterdam's city center during the aerial attack by the Luftwaffe.
Opposite right: Canal houses in Rotterdam suffered severe damage as well, some of which were centuries old.
Principal picture: German parachutists descend on the Dutch capital, The Hague, a few miles from Rotterdam on 10 May.**

Left: German tanks roll across the grassy, rolling plains of Belgium in the first stages of Blitzkrieg 1940.

frustrated German plans, but also made it possible when all hope to further struggle was lost, for the Queen, the Royal Family and the government to escape to Britain.

The following day, 12 May, there occurred the first encounter between the German forces and those of its principal antagonists. Giraud's Seventh Army, racing to form a junction between Dutch and Belgian lines, was surprised near Tilburg just inside Holland. Caught off-balance while on the move, it was forced to withdraw and took up a line, Breda-St Leonard, astride the frontiers.

By the next evening the 9th Panzer Division reached the paratroops on the Moerdijk. There was now, therefore, a continuous German line running across Holland from frontier to coast. With the enemy wheeling around across their rear, the commanders of the forward Dutch units were compelled to order a speedy withdrawal into Fortress Holland on the night of 13/14th.

Despite the holdup which had occurred to their plans for The Hague, German intentions were now largely fulfilled and all that remained was to complete the isolation of the Dutch forces and then bring the struggle in the north to a speedy conclusion. The first step in this direction took place on 14 May. The key to Fortress Holland lay through Rotterdam, with its concentration of road and rail links into the heartland. The attackers were now poised on the southern edge of the city and in fact, as later events proved, they could simply have advanced from these positions on the 13th or early on the 14th and would have encountered little resistance. Instead they dropped an ultimatum threatening obliteration by air bombardment if the garrison did not surrender.

The ultimatum, handed over at 1320, gave three hours for a decision to be taken. To the astonished horror of the inhabitants of Rotterdam, scarcely had it been received than two groups, each of twenty-seven planes, began gathering over the city and unleashing high explosives and incendiaries. Within minutes the entire city was ablaze and some 900 of its citizens lay dead or wounded. Over the subsequent days, the Dutch authorities had, added to their other burdens, to try to bring help to the stricken city while refugees from it and other places clogged roads needed by the army for its own movements.

The international outcry against this German act was such that Goebbels, the

Left: German soldier camouflages his lookout position. Adequate cover was difficult to achieve.

Above: A Dornier Do-17 bomber, the 'Flying Pencil,' over the Low Countries.

German propaganda chief, was forced to answer it. He first tried to claim that it had resulted from the Dutch commander's ignoring the ultimatum; later he declared that it was the work of the Royal Air Force and when neither explanations proved convincing, sought to show the damage was actually minimal and that only military targets had been hit.

The reason for this barbarous act has never been clear. Some confusion may have resulted from the fact that there were actually two ultimata delivered to the Dutch commander. The first, handed over at 1030, was unsigned and therefore returned. It had set a two-hour deadline so that the raid would have come at 1230, a time particularly popular with the Luftwaffe as the one when the maximum number of people were on the streets. The signed version was not handed over until nearly an hour after this and no attackers had appeared over Rotterdam up to that time. It is plain, therefore, that the postponement had been communicated to the air force.

Why was it, then, that only two minutes after reception of the second ultimatum

the raid began? Communications failure is one answer. Once in the air the only means of communication from the ground was by means of flares and the German commander in south Rotterdam, to his eternal credit, released flare after flare in an effort to prevent the calamity. Either they were not seen or there is another explanation. This is that German High Command or, as some say, Göring himself, had ordered the raid to go ahead regardless as an example of what would happen to other Dutch cities if the struggle

were not abandoned. In favor of this thesis is the fact that aircraft not due to attack until 1620 hours (the second ultimatum, handed over at 1330 set a three-hour deadline) were actually over the city hours before this. In actions of this kind, the Luftwaffe prided itself on arriving to the second.

Oberkommando des Heeres (OKH) planning had allowed one day for the conquest of Holland. It had so far taken four. Although it had been possible for the attackers to deploy over the plain of

Right: A camouflaged German soldier in the marshy area between the Mass and Waal Rivers.

Parachutists

The first major parachute drop of the war created an advance spearhead for the invading Germans. The drops over Holland failed in their first objective for the most part, since many were captured. But the psychological effect of being caught by surprise was devastating and helped bring swift victory to Germany. The photographs on this page show the various stages of a parachute raid over Holland from Ju-52 transports. The bottom right picture shows how one parachutist was caught on a bridge and had to be rescued.

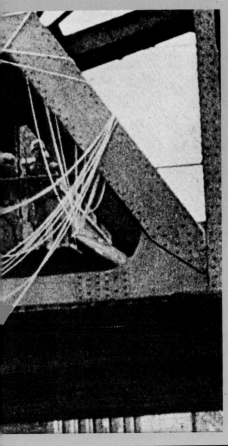

Brabant and, under airborne attack, Fortress Holland had proved itself far less defensible than had been supposed; in other places determined resistance was holding back the onslaught. The Zuiderzee dike was retained by a combination of military and naval forces with the Royal Navy and the French fleet giving assistance. In Zeeland, too, the Dutch troops were still holding a line.

In the overall context of the war, the period of Dutch resistance might perhaps seem negligible, it is nonetheless a tribute to the sacrificial bravery of a small country and its forces. And the price had been truly appalling. Some units had lost as much as eight percent of their effectives — a proportion far too high to be tolerated in view of the army's size.

After the bombing of Rotterdam and when the great historic city of Utrecht was threatened with similar treatment, consideration had to be given to the justification for continuing a struggle whose cost was so immense.

The Dutch Commander in Chief, General Winkelman, had indicated that considerable help would be needed from the Allies if the country was to fight on, as it was prepared to do. Queen Wilhelmina and her family were now in Britain, living in apartments at Buckingham Palace put at her disposal by the British sovereign. She addressed a personal appeal to him, while members of her government, also now in London, appealed separately to the British General Staff and directly to Churchill, and a telegram was sent to the French president.

It was obvious that no one was in a position to offer help on the scale required and the Dutch commander could only be instructed to act at his own discretion. At 1650 on the 15th, therefore, Winkelman, in an effort to save further useless effusion of blood, particularly among the civil population, telexed all units to stop fighting after first destroying arms and ammunition. Bock's Army Group B had succeeded in its objectives and was now free to turn its forces southward.

In Belgium, now that the advanced delaying line on the Albert Canal was untenable, the defenders were pulling back to another one further back, still hoping to hold the enemy while the Dyle positions were occupied. Their movement was attended by the greatest difficulty as in some places roving German Panzers had moved behind the defenders' front. However, no real attempt was made to exploit this advantage and they were able to take refuge behind the River Gette, already held by a French covering force. With rearguards holding advanced positions, a general retreat towards the 'Dyle Plan' positions then took place.

The British and French, knowing that with the capture of Eben Emael time was against them, were hurrying to consolidate. Next to the Belgians and to the

north of Wavre was the British Expeditionary Force, whose first units had arrived on the evening of the 10th and began digging in in full strength on the morning of the 17th. To their right was the French Army Group 1 under Billotte, whose sector extended down to the Maginot shoulder. This consisted of fourteen infantry divisions, one light mechanized and four of cavalry. To the north of the BEF and the Belgians was the French Seventh, which as we know had come under attack while on the march and was prevented from helping the Dutch.

Of all the enemy weapons, the one which would cause otherwise determined and well-disciplined forces most often to wither and collapse was the Stuka dive bomber, Junkers 87. As later experience was to show, when the Royal Air Force virtually shot it out of the sky, it was far from being an aeronautical masterpiece. It had tricks of its own which its pilots dreaded and outstanding weaknesses which made it vulnerable to attack even from the ground. It was, however, as much a psychological as a tactical weapon and indeed its accuracy was poor. In its dive it emitted a scream, thanks to a siren, an idea dreamed up by its main designer, Ernst Udet. Its unnerving sound was replaced by the whistle of its bomb as it slung it forward like a projectile in the upward swing out of the dive. Seconds later came the crash of the explosion. Thus a massed Stuka attack, unpleasant enough in itself, was made the more hideous by this succession of noises as much as by its appearance like a bird of prey with outstretched talons. A man under its attack, even a veteran, would speak of the terrifying feeling that it was coming for him, personally; after frequent subjection to it, he would become a pale, trembling wreck who could infect others with his own dread long before they had encountered its reality.

Lacking the one thing which would have reduced the scale of the menace, air power, the Allies looked for palliatives including the use of earplugs and rubber-bungs held in the mouth to prevent the conduction of shock waves to brain. None of the possible solutions was ever adopted on more than an experimental scale, so that the troops simply had to tolerate, or as so often happened, break under it, demoralized even before the ruthless steel monsters, the flame-throwing tanks they dreaded almost as much, came to sniff them out and spit their dragon's-fire over them. In practice the French suffered more than the British, since the former were not trained to dig the slit trenches which it had been shown gave adequate protection, and were constantly caught in open ground.

On the afternoon of the 12th French troops were for the first time exposed to

it, but when it was followed by an attack from the XVI Panzer Corps between Tirlemont (Tienen) and Huy, the defenders stood their ground. This was the only contact with the enemy, save for encounters with his reconnaissance units.

In fact the German Fourth Army which was operating in this sector had failed to follow up its advantages because the attackers were experiencing confusions of their own. Two of their armies, the Sixth and Eighteenth, were having difficulties finding one another, leaving a gap with only thin forces along it.

However, the Allies quickly realized that there was no administrative cohesion between the armies of the three nations, now participating in the struggle. Typical of the problem was an incident on 10 May when a British and a Belgian division were both ordered to occupy the same sector of the Louvain line.

Above: A ground mechanic of the Luftwaffe with an ammunition belt.
Above right: The cockpit of a Junkers Ju-88 bomber.
Below: A Ju-52 transport paratroops carrier which was shot down over Holland.

To try to obviate such occurrences, a conference was called at Casteau near Mons on the afternoon of 10 May. Those present included King Leopold, titular Commander in Chief of the Belgian forces; Edouard Daladier, since his supercession as premier by Reynaud, Minister of War; General Georges, commanding Northeast Front; General Billotte, commanding Army Group 1; and General Sir Henry Pownall, Chief of Staff of the BEF. The solution here adopted was that Billotte should act as delegate of General Georges in co-ordinating the actions of all the Allies in Belgium. As was quickly proved, the appointment was meaningless, since Billotte was fully occupied with the operations of his own army group and had no time to devote to inter-Allied liaison. Both the Belgian command and that of the BEF were left virtually to their own devices, though strongly criti-

Above: A squadron of Focke-Wulf Fw-200 Condor bombers shortly before take-off.

cized when their desperate efforts resulted in disaster as was often the case.

One result of the Casteau meeting was, however, that the British were given the Louvain sector, though the failure to resolve the underlying problem was demonstrated three days later, at the height of a major battle involving troops of all three nations. Liaison between a French Light Mechanized Division and the Belgian forces disintegrated.

The attack of 13 May began with the usual Stuka raid, the chosen arena being a sector Hannut–Merdorp–Jandrain in the Tirlemont–Liège–Namur triangle. At 1100 hours an artillery bombardment was followed by the dive bombers falling out of the sky in screaming attack after attack. Following the pattern used in Poland and soon to become standard in the west, they were succeeded by the tanks of the 3rd and 4th Panzer Divisions, advancing *en masse*, surrounding the defensive points and reducing them, breaking through wherever there was an opening and this way reaching round the flanks into the rear of the defense. Whenever a way was blocked to them they simply swung on squeaking tracks and

rolled off to find another. As the defenders' strongpoints fell, the infantry followed up, destroying the last pockets of resistance and consolidating gains.

The French armored force under General Prioux, a brave, intelligent and resourceful officer, respected on all sides, bore the brunt of the attack and his men fought back with leonine courage. Nevertheless by 1745, their positions overrun, they were forced to pull back to Perwez, where the Belgians had constructed a formidable antitank obstacle which it was hoped could be held.

In point of fact, here, as on several subsequent occasions, the French had at their disposal a force of tanks at least equal to the German one and had they

Above right: A bombed-out Dutch Army barracks near The Hague.
Far right: Wehrmacht troops crouch behind their artillery as they root out defenders of Scheveningen.
Below: Motorized Dutch forces on a dike in South Holland.
Right: Bewildered Rotterdamers watch helplessly as German troops occupy their damaged city.

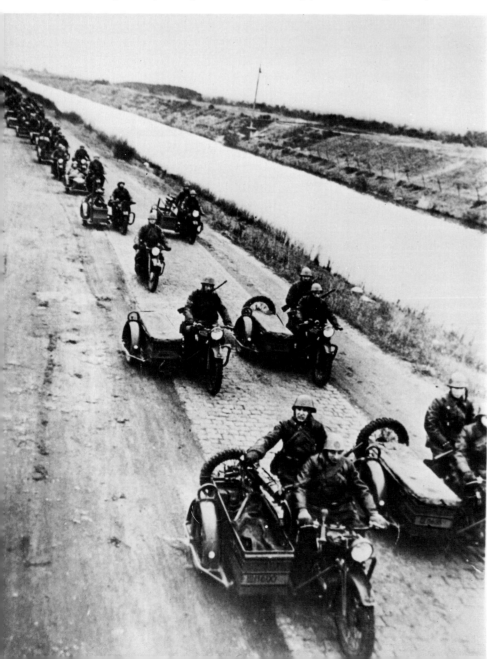

Above: Ju-88 bomber crew suits up for a night raid.
Below: Scenes from a German propaganda film depicting the round-up of Dutch POWs.

been concentrated in parks within reach of the threatened area they could certainly have turned the tide of battle. As it was, those tanks which did take part, though they inflicted heavy enough losses, were finally incapacitated by the concentration on them of overwhelming numbers and many had to be abandoned on the field of battle.

Notwithstanding this defeat, over the night 13/14 May the Allied armies were forming a solid line. Giraud's Seventh Army was along the south bank of the Scheldt covering with its right wing the approaches of Antwerp. From here the line bent obliquely toward the south running down to Louvain where the Belgian forces were ranged in echelons of eight divisions, three, three and two, with the cavalry and a division of Chasseurs Ardennais in reserve. From Louvain down to Wavre were the nine divisions of the BEF, disposed in depth with their reserves and placed so they could be moved rapidly to any threatened sector.

Next to the British were the six divisions of the French First Army (as part of Army Group 1), with two mechanized divisions in reserve. Namur itself was held by two Belgian divisions who had the guns of the fortress to support them.

For all their strength, however, the Allied dispositions were still, in German eyes, the left arm which they hoped soon to lop from the shoulder. In any event they were soon to be rendered impotent by the blow to the stomach.

In war, as in so much else in human life, there are no certainties. The trap might be set, but there is no guarantee that the quarry will walk into it. The danger for the Germans was that the Allies might decide on a rapid sidestep southward, back to their original and stronger line. Had they done so, they would also have placed themselves firmly along the flanks of Rundstedt's Army Group A which had

Below: The Bridge over the Ijssel River at Zutphen after it had been blown up by the Germans. This area of central and eastern Holland fell within the first two days of the Blitzkrieg.

begun advancing toward the French coast, the first lunging for the belly, an operation which for all the glitter of its prizes was still fraught with risk. It was essential that the French First Army and the other forces, Belgian and British, should not be able to go to the aid of the French Ninth about to be threatened.

On the night of 14 May, Reichenau, commanding the Sixth Army operating on the right wing of Army Group B, was ordered to attack the enemy troops in the Louvain-Namur area, his actions having the objective of preventing their consolidation while at the same time doing nothing which would force a general withdrawal and hence their use as reinforcement for the Ninth Army.

Once more the following day the French were subjected to the assaults of the 3rd and 4th Panzer Divisions with the axis toward Gembloux on the Brussels-Namur trunk road. The defenders withstood, though they had already lost their reserves in the battle in the south.

The same day the British 3rd Division at Louvain came under attack and was forced back, allowing the German forces to penetrate the city which had suffered so greatly twenty-five years earlier. But the Germans had come up against a British commander they were later to know so well — Bernard Montgomery. In the afternoon he ordered his troops to counterattack under cover of a sustained bombardment and dislodged the enemy.

That evening, however, the Army Group 1 commander, Billotte, was primarily concerned with the right flank after the breakthrough in the south toward the sea by Army Group A. Accordingly he decided on 15 May to abandon the entire

Dyle line and move his forces as far out of reach as possible.

In ordering this extensive withdrawal, Billotte could be (and was) accused of panic reaction, particularly since his own forces had stood their ground, while along the British sector the Germans had actually been pushed out of their gains at Louvain. On the other hand Billotte's immediate superior, Georges, at Northeast Front, was also overreacting, while, by sheer contrast, at GHQ there seemed to be absolutely no understanding of the magnitude of events and of the threat developing. At French headquarters in the bleak fortress of Vincennes where Mata Hari had faced the firing squad in 1917, Gamelin seemed to be intent on avoiding the trap into which his World War I chief, Joffre, had fallen. Whenever he had departed from a policy called with more generosity than justice one of 'masterly

Above: A rudimentary road sign scrawled by the SS in Holland.
Left: The port of Rotterdam.

Above: Advancing German troops pass a Dutch windmill.

inactivity,' he had brought immediate disaster. Gamelin had apparently decided to confine himself to the 'masterly inactivity.' Thus one tier of the complex French command system was in panic while the next was inert.

It was little wonder that Billotte himself pursued a somewhat erratic course. But to make the situation worse, now withdrawal had been decided on, such was the state of communications that the Belgian and British commanders, who

Left: A PzKw-1 German tank of the type used extensively in all early Blitzkriegs.

were intimately involved, learned of it only by accident when liaison officers were reading through orders at Billotte's HQ before their promulgation.

What was more, the Belgians had their own internal communications difficulties. Their army's GHQ was operating under peculiar difficulty. It had been situated in Bruges, nearer to Ostend than Brussels, and infinitely more remote from the front. No doubt, in siting it so near the coast the Belgians had in mind that their Commander in Chief, since he was also their King, would be in a better position to flee if necessary to head a government in exile. Nonetheless the disadvantage of remoteness was increased by the fact the headquarters was accommodated in an old castle, itself in the country and

surrounded by a moat. Telephone and other communications were poor and the only reliable way of conveying information was by dispatch rider. In such circumstances, a speedy reaction was hardly to be hoped for.

The withdrawal now planned was. a complicated one. It was to be carried out in three stages on the night of the 16th, and covered by rearguards along the Willebroek Canal, the Senne and Dender Rivers. At the same time the French Seventh

Above left: The freshly planted grave of a Dutch soldier.
Above: Mourners pass the graves of Dutch soldiers killed in action.
Below: Wrecked Dutch fishing boats were among the many victims of Blitzkrieg 1940.

Army, previously in the far north, was now ordered south. Thus it would be moving in this direction while the retreating forces from the Dyle were moving westward. The result was total chaos made worse by the fact that although there was no concentrated enemy attack, there was continual harassment.

The entire episode was demonstrative of organizational failure from top to bottom. Had the Germans known of this and struck vigorously, the slaughter would have been immense. Mercifully they seemed to have been struck with lethargy and did not follow it up. Bock was later to claim that this was contrary to his own inclinations, but that the Chief of Staff at OKH (Army High Command, not to be confused with OKW, Oberkommando der Wehrmacht or High Command of the Armed Forces), General Halder, a notoriously hesitant man, wanted to restrict Bock's role to a purely protective one on the right flank. Seeing that the main struggle was in the south Halder even deprived him of the XVI Panzer Corps, plus its bridging units essential to pursuit in this region of rivers and canals.

Even on the 17th, when the attack was resumed the lack of them hampered movement, as one German general said, more than the enemy. However, on the 19th a surprise thrust took them into Antwerp after crossing the Scheldt, while elsewhere the Chasseur Ardennais were involved in bitter fighting along the Dender.

Realization of precisely what was happening now reached all levels of French society. Gamelin, it is true, continued to face events with equanimity. That day Reynaud had sent out a message recalling two old *Soldats de France*. One was Philippe Pétain, the eighty-four-year-old hero of Verdun, at the time Ambassador in Madrid, to whom he offered the vice-premiership. The other was Maxime Weygand, commanding the French Forces in the Middle East from Beirut, rabidly anti-Left and pro such right-wing manifestations as Catholic Action. Now seventy-three, though he looked younger than his years, he had once been described by a compatriot as one of those rare cases where the mind ages before the body, instead of the reverse.

On 20 May he moved to Vincennes where his first act was to cancel all Gamelin's orders for a riposte to the enemy attacks.

Above left: A German bomber shot
down by Dutch AA fire.
Above: Dutch soldiers taken
prisoner by the Germans in Rotterdam the day of the aerial attack,
14 May.
Above right: Queen Wilhelmina
arrives in London on 15 May
carrying her own steel helmet. She
formed the Dutch government-in-
exile upon her arrival.
Right: Another Luftwaffe aircraft
that did not make it back from
Holland.
Below: The Dutch ship *Pieter Koen*
which was sunk off the North Sea
coast by aerial attack.

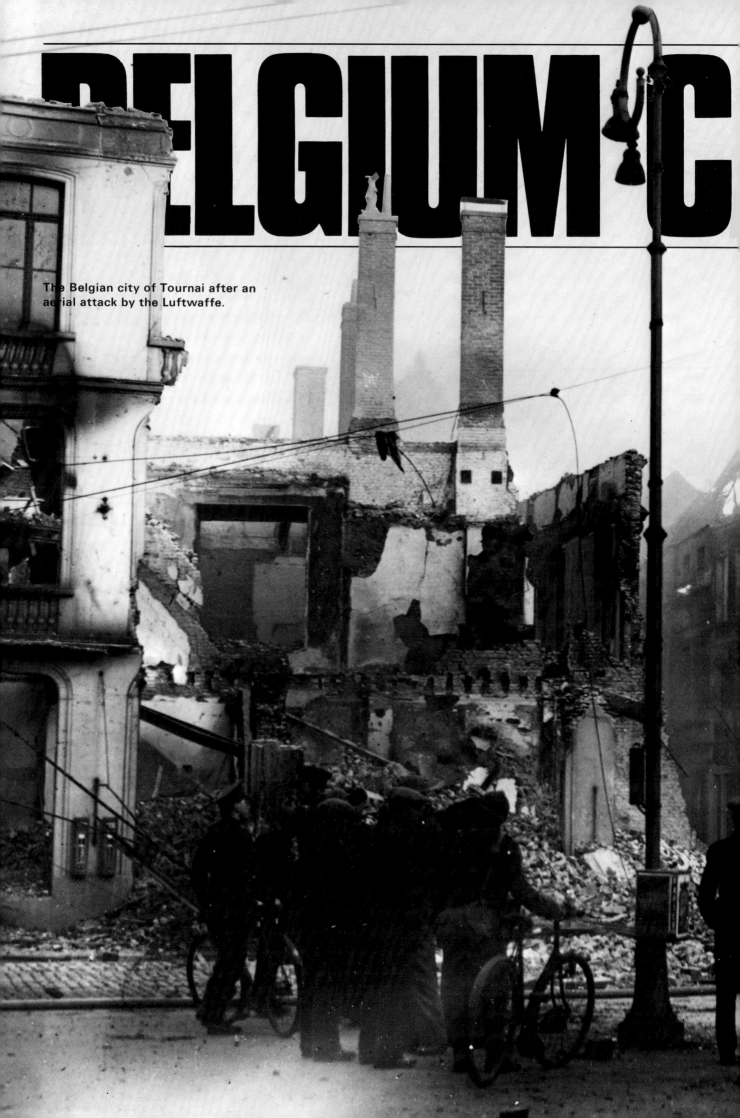

BELGIUM C

The Belgian city of Tournai after an aerial attack by the Luftwaffe.

PITULATION

BLITZKRIEG
1940

Belgium,
20-28 May 1940

For a moment it was as if Weygand had been touched by the shade of his former chief, Foch, who had a reputation for coming on the scene when all was lost and saving the situation. Certainly in the period immediately following his appointment there seemed to be an improvement in the Allied position.

By 20 May King Leopold's distant headquarters could feel happy in the knowledge that if all else had gone badly, the withdrawal had been completed according to plan and without major mishaps. The armies occupied a line from Terneuzen in Holland, opposite Zeeland, down to Oudenarde (Audenard) on the Scheldt. It was held with eleven divisions with a further seven in reserve. From Oudenarde down, the British Expeditionary Force were next it line with seven divisions in line and one in reserve. However, Gort, concerned lest there should be a sudden and unwarned withdrawal of the French First Army on his right, decided to secure his own positions by giving himself all round cover and installed units down as far as La Bassée Canal. He placed outposts at intervals along the canal as far as the coast and so behind the First Army.

There was only one snag. Rundstedt's attempt to cut off the northern armies had succeeded: their Panzers had reached the coast. The forces in Belgium and those in France were isolated from one another.

It was this crisis which led the Chief of the Imperial General Staff, General Ironside, to fly to France and confer with Lord Gort and the French Army Group 1 commander, Billotte. What was discussed was a plan for slicing through the German flank thereby uniting the separated forces. This, however, was an operation which properly belongs to another aspect of the story, that of the whole struggle for France, and will be told later.

This indeed was a time of conferences. Weygand conceived it as his first duty to

**Above: Hitler poses proudly with the paratroops who seized Fort Eben Emael.
Below: Hitler visits Bastogne after its seizure by the Wehrmacht. The Führer is driven by his aide Kempka; his adjutant Schmundt stands behind.**

Left: Hitler explains his plans for the second stage of Blitzkrieg from his Belgian headquarters surrounded by Ernst Udet (far left) and Göring and Bormann (right).

**Left: Hitler interviews three para-
troops who took Eben Emael.
Right: Polish troops in the main
square of Arras after the
presentation of new colors.**

visit the front commanders and gain a
first-hand picture of conditions. The
culmination of this tour, which he hoped
would become a regular feature of his
command, was to be a conference with
the Commanders in Chief of the armies of
all three nations. The first of these was to
be held at Ypres.

His journey itself should have been
indicative of how affairs stood. At Le
Bourget in Paris no one knew anything
about either his flight or his plane. When
he and his ADC arrived at their destination, the airport near Béthune, they found
it deserted. As Weygand himself writes,
'The General who had just been invested
with the command of all theaters of
operations . . . found himself . . . alone in
the countryside.' Finally they managed to
hitch a lift on a truck to the nearest
telephone office.

When at last he arrived, at another
hurriedly arranged location, he found only
King Leopold and his personal military
adviser, General van Overstraeten, present.
Billotte turned up later, but Gort missed
this crucial meeting with the new Allied
Commander in Chief and thus was the
recipient of decisions.

Weygand explained that it was his
conviction that the armies in the north
should go over to the offensive as soon
as possible. To make sufficient force
available for this, the line would have to
be shortened which entailed further with-
drawals. In particular, the Belgians were
to be coralled behind the River Ijzer.

According to some sources, it was only
in the subsequent discussion that Weygand learned that the northern armies
were actually cut off. This is contradicted
by the General himself, who writes of his
aircraft *en route* for Ypres being fired at
from guns on the coast 'which confirmed
that the Germans had reached the sea.'

What did emerge, however, was that
the Belgians would withdraw no further.
Van Overstraeten, on their behalf, pointed
out that his men were tired, the rear
congested with refugees and that the
effect on morale of further retirement
would be disastrous, remembering that
many of the men would be giving up their
homes, the very places for which they
were supposed to be fighting. Weygand
was therefore forced to concede that they
should hold their present lines, provided
that some way of freeing the British divisions for his offensive could be found. It

**Above left: General Guderian in
Belgium in May 1940.
Left: French colonial troops
captured by the Germans in
Belgium.**

**Left: British forces move up to the front through a Belgian town.
Above: Belgian refugees are evacuated from the war zone.**

was finally agreed that the Belgians should extend their front southward for this purpose, a singularly hazardous undertaking in view of their waning will to resist. These points decided, Weygand took his leave and struggled back to Paris.

When Gort arrived, some time later but before the others had left, the reason for his delay was at once plain: a fresh disaster had befallen the defenders as the Germans had crossed the Scheldt near

Below: British light tank passes triumphantly through the same Belgian town.

Oudenarde and immediate steps needed to be taken to avoid a gap in the line. In his view, the only course was withdrawal behind the Lys, nearer to the Belgian coast. At 2000 hours the conference broke up having decided on this action.

Gort regarded Weygand's plan for an offensive as little more than a pipe dream. The requisite strength simply did not exist. Nonetheless, in the interests of inter-Allied co-operation he undertook to provide three divisions for it. But whichever way the sums were done, the numbers remained pitifully small and under the present scheme amounted to a mere five divisions.

Then, as the principals went their separate ways, another mishap occurred. Billotte, bearer of the common decisions to his own forces, was fatally injured in a

road accident. General Blanchard, Commander of the First Army, was appointed to succeed him, but it was not until midday on the 22nd, that he was finally apprised of the plan.

Discussions of the situation were also going on the other side at OKH. Here the army Commander in Chief, Field-Marshal Walther von Brauchitsch, was urging an all-out effort to complete the envelopment and annihilation of the enemy forces in the north. Since he believed those in the south posed little threat he wanted von Rundstedt's Army Group A to reinforce Army Group B to achieve a rapid result. But Rundstedt, now almost sixty-four, was of an older school of German

Below: British transport passes across the Franco–Belgian border.

British tanks and Bren-gun carriers pass through the ruins of Louvain, which was not spared in either of the two world wars.

**Above: Belgian soldiers enthusi-
astically greet the Tommies as they
advanced into the Belgian pocket.**

officers, indeed with the duelling scars on
his cheeks was almost the archetypal
figure of the German general so beloved
of the Allied cartoonists. For all that he
had shown himself flexible enough in
adapting to the new modes of warfare,
there was still a streak of caution which
recoiled from undue boldness. Furthermore he believed he might at any time
come under attack from the French
Seventh Army and, as we shall see, had
already been attacked by the British. He
now felt that his armor was too far ahead
of the infantry and wanted the gap
reduced. He therefore decided to regroup

on a line Gravelines–St Omer–Bethune
along the Aa Canal, halting to do so and
thereby giving the British an unexpected
chance to strengthen their defenses.

If communication was bad in the
French and Belgian Armies, it was scarcely
better in the German so that Brauchitsch
was totally unaware of what Rundstedt
was doing. Pursuing his conviction that
the first thing was to liquidate the
remaining forces in the north, he accordingly ordered the transfer of Klüge's
Fourth Army from Rundstedt's Army
Group to Bock's to strengthen it.

The defenders of the pocket would
now have the enemy advancing on them
from two sides, closing off the only
escape route remaining, the seaward one.
It chanced, however, that on the 24th

**Above: Streams of refugees march
down Belgian roads into France,
carrying a few personal belongings.
Right: British Bren carriers pause
as Belgian refugees force them into
a temporary detour.**

Hitler was paying a visit to von Rundstedt's headquarters and was there told of
Brauchitsch's order just eight and half
hours before it was to come into effect.
His response was to cancel it and the
assault on two sides was abandoned.

During this respite, the encircled Allied
forces went ahead with their regroupment
as agreed at the conference. This was
done more or less without major incident,
though movement was made difficult by
the hordes of refugees, and the Luftwaffe,

with almost unchallenged air superiority, subjected them to constant harassment.

The line was now very roughly the shape of a thick, inverted letter L. Its base line ran along the coast, Belgian and French. The inner edge of this base line was held by the Belgian Army up to the Menin–Halluin area. Hereafter forming the inner side of the upright of the L (and thus at right angles to the Belgians) was the British sector, running southward down to below Annappes. Beyond this point the French First Army held a defense line forming the top of the L with its termini at Maulde and Marchiennes, and continuing up as far as Thumeries. The outer side of the upright line back to the coast was again held by British forces. This upright, in which the defenders stood, as it were, back-to-back, was not only difficult to protect but also produced an overextended line. It existed because between the two fronts was the important industrial city of Lille which the French command as well as the politicians were most anxious not to relinquish. In any case loss of this area would vastly increase the gap between the armies on either side of the German line and so affect their ability to reach one another.

It was from most points of view a

Left: A British anti-tank position in the ruins of Louvain.
Below: Belgian civilians welcome British armored vehicles as they advance into the Belgian pocket.

restricted and uncomfortable line to defend, proferring a number of weak points to the enemy. The Germans, it was plain, did not intend to allow their advantage to go by default. To make their dominance abundantly clear they dropped leaflets on the defenders showing them just how small was the area now held and how feeble any hope they might entertain of continued resistance. By the 23rd the Eighteenth Army which had been fighting in Holland swung round to face the northern tip of the Belgian line. That evening infiltrators began breaking into the bridgehead around Ghent.

Following a withdrawal from here, the Belgian front ran from Menin behind the Lys to the junction with the Lys Canal at Deinze which it followed up to the sea at Zeebrugge. The river was little protection since it was only thirty meters at its widest and its water level was low. Furthermore the region was one of dikes while the river itself twisted and meandered making the line over-long.

Menin, where the Belgian line was attached to the British in the crook of the L, seemed the most likely place for the Germans to concentrate their efforts, if possible dividing the armies of the two nations. This was confirmed when units from Montgomery's 3rd Division carried out a raid far behind the German lines and captured orders to their Fourth Army which revealed their intention to do this.

On the night of 23/24 May artillery began bombarding the line from Menin

Above: A Belgian home devastated by German bombing. Destruction was far less severe in 1940 than it was in 1914.

up to Courtrai with the dreaded Stukas striking at rear communications. In the afternoon of the 24th the attack came with four divisions streaming across the Lys on either side of Courtrai and breaking through in the sector of the line held by the Belgian 1st and 3rd Divisions. The gap was filled, though only by using the last remaining reserves.

In view of the attack's location, the

Left: Belgian civilians and soldiers greet advancing British transports. Above: British soldiers adjust their gas capes in the ruins of a Belgian town.

British command was also deeply concerned. Penetration here would leave the BEF with its flank open at the point where it joined the Belgian sector. The enemy could swing southward and so into the British rear, cutting them off from the coast and escape. On 24 May Gort decided there was only one possible course of action and this was to use the 5th and 50th Divisions (being held for the breakout attack toward the south) to take up positions along a line behind the Ijzer from Comines, through Ypres to Boesinghe.

The decision, as we shall see later, was one fraught with consequences for the planned counteroffensive, but it was taken in the consciousness that Belgian resistance was reaching its end and that it was necessary to secure in advance what would then remain of the Allied pocket. The growing seriousness of the Belgian situation was plain from the note of desperation detectable in the Order of the Day issued by King Leopold on 25 May. 'Soldiers,' it read, 'the great battle which we have been expecting has begun. It will be fierce. We will fight on with all

our strength and with supreme energy. It is being fought on the ground where in 1914 we victoriously held the invader. Soldiers, Belgium expects you to do honor to the Flag. Officers, soldiers, whatever may happen, I shall share your fate. I call on you for firmness, discipline and confidence. Our cause is pure and just. Providence will help us. Long live Belgium!'

That morning at 0700 hours the Germans had broken through and formed a new bridgehead at Deinze, the junction of the Lys River and Canal. Some of the more disaffected units fell back, but the Chasseurs Ardennais fought back fiercely, depriving the enemy attack of its momentum. This notwithstanding, there were two ominous salients in the defense line — one on either side of Courtrai and the other round Deinze.

Taking advantage of the position at Courtrai, the Germans attacked toward Iseghem, crossed the Mandel Canal at Ingelmunster and, swinging northward, joined up with the second bridgehead round Deinze. Further north still, the canal line was forced above Eeklo. At the same time the rear civilian and military were being terrorized by air attack. Refugees scuttled from one place to another, seeking vainly for a sanctuary and, in doing so, blocking the roads.

Almost incredibly a continuous line

was maintained by somehow plugging every gap as it was formed — a tribute to the enormous bravery of the Belgian troops. However, the situation was not one which could possibly endure. Army headquarters was being swamped with requests for reinforcements as crises began to develop at no fewer than six different points along the front. It had little to offer beyond the remnants of three divisions, themselves badly mauled. What was worse, the defenders were losing their equipment at a phenomenal rate because, as the envelopment of their positions was threatened, units could only extricate themselves by abandoning their heavy weapons.

On 26 May the King sent warning of his Army's plight. The limits of resistance had practically been reached. There were, furthermore, no forces available to block the enemy advance on Ypres while a withdrawal to the Ijzer was now out of the question since it would have involved the army in greater losses than a setpiece battle.

From early on the 27th the attack was renewed with the main enemy thrusts falling on the Belgian center toward Thielt (Tielt). By noon a five-mile-wide gap had been punched in the line, and this time there was nothing left to fill the gap. Half an hour later Leopold warned both Gort and the French that collapse

Above: General Keitel, Hitler, General Jodl, and Martin Bormann at the Führer's Belgian head-quarters in May 1940.

was imminent. That morning the King had been visited by Admiral Keyes, head of the British military mission, bearing a message from the British King begging him to leave the country and to continue to lead Belgian resistance from England. After consideration, he refused. His place, he insisted, was with his own people.

After leaving the King, Keyes telephoned London. He reported that Belgian resistance was at its end that the King had refused the offer of sanctuary. Churchill pressed him to try again.

At 1600 hours it was decided to send out a truce mission. Allied representatives at Belgian headquarters were informed of this, and while the situation was accepted by the British official, which of course had already realized its inevitability, his French counterpart protested volubly that before a truce was accepted all three nations should be called in to state their views and no action be taken without common consent. At this stage such arguments were academic, though the Belgians pointed out that they were simply inquiring about terms, not taking irrevocable decisions.

However, when Weygand received the telegram informing him what had occurred, he signalled Army Group 1: 'The French and British governments are

agreed to order General Blanchard and Lord Gort to defend the honor of their flags by dissociating themselves completely with the Belgian Army.' That text, redundant anyway — it was not for a moment suggested that British or French units were to be surrendered — was a gratuitous insult to a brave ally. The Belgians had shown in 1940, as they had in 1914, that they were not unconscious of the meaning of honor.

By this time, anyway, the Belgian Deputy Chief of Staff, Major General Derousseaux, was trying to find his way toward the German lines and eventually reached the command post of an Army Corps' general who passed on the message to OKH. The answer he received was unambiguous: Hitler would accept only unconditional surrender.

That act was one of many sidelights on the dictator's character. He was the ineffable bully, as lacking in sensitivity as in grace. The Belgians, tiny as their nation is, had fought both bravely and chivalrously against one they could have no hope of defeating. They deserved magnanimity, not humiliation. In German eyes they had committed the unpardonable sin of being weak.

At 2300 hours, within half an hour of Derousseaux's returning to his own headquarters, it was decided that there was no alternative to acceptance. At the same time the King again refused Keyes's invitation to come to Britain. The admiral left and, with his staff, tried to find a way

of escape. In the end they had to leave by fishing boat, but were picked up by a British torpedo boat and taken to Harwich.

In Belgium a few formalities remained. The French 60th Division which had been under Belgian command had to be handed over and was moved across the Ijzer in trucks. At 0400 hours on 28 May firing along the Belgian lines ceased with the exception of some units in the south, around the Ypres-Roulers sectors who were without communication and who fought on until 0600.

News of the Belgian surrender came as a surprise to the French government because, due to the failure of their communications, the warning messages had never been received. Reynaud, the French Prime Minister, on hearing it, was thrown into a fury and could never forgive the British who refused to see the Belgians as traitors to the Allied cause.

This anger largely focussed on King Leopold, accused by the French of arrant cowardice, as though he had handed over intact an unblooded army. Many of the accusations made against him were to survive. Members of the Belgian government, those lions of courage who had insisted on waiting until the enemy was inside their gates before taking measures of defense, insisted that the royal decision to capitulate was made without their consent.

At the time and subsequently, rumors about the King were rife which can only be compared with the scurrilous stories

Right: Part of the destruction of a Belgian town.

about the Russian Tsarina circulated just before the Revolution. It was suggested that he had been the creature of the Germans. There were even legends that the motor accident in which his first wife, Astrid of Sweden, was killed had been engineered by the Gestapo as the means of getting their own emissaries into the court. It is hard to square these with both Leopold and his Army's conduct during the period of its resistance. All the same, when he announced his intention of returning to the throne after the war, such was the outcry that he was forced to abdicate in favor of his son, Baudouin.

It is easy enough to understand the feelings aroused at the time both by the surrender and by the King's decision to stay in Belgium where, obviously, he could be of no further service to the Allied cause. At the same time, by the more charitable light of hindsight, one must also see that he was placed in an appalling quandary. Certainly the temptation to leave must have been strong: his own dynasty had links with the British Royal Family and he was educated at Eton. At the same time can it not be cogently argued that in times of such crisis for his country, the place of the head of state is among his own people? Nor was the decision without courage in itself. Since the Germans had demanded nothing less than unconditional surrender, his own fate was most uncertain. In fact as we know he was kept in internment at Laeken near Brussels throughout the war.

As for his decision to surrender, one has to see that the Belgian forces, save for isolated instances, fought bravely and added a lustrous page to their country's history. If they were defeated, it was because they were not only outnumbered but also outwitted – like their Allies, they had prepared for the wrong war.

It could still be argued that their defection had weakened the position of the embattled garrison north of von Rundstedt's line. It is hard to see how their continuing to fight and die could have greatly affected the issue. Even the German forces they were engaging were comparatively small in number.

On the contrary an ally in extremis can often be a greater danger than help, since he cannot be relied upon to hold what are perhaps crucial positions and may make demands for assistance his partners can only respond to at their peril. Gort's forces, which, as we have seen, had been anticipating events, had already prepared their positions and could now accept with equanimity, if not enthusiasm, that they were on their own.

Right: Queen Wilhelmina of Holland and Belgian King Leopold III in happier days in 1939.

THE REAPER

A PzKw-IV L-24 German tank in France in May 1940.

S GO FORTH

For all that it had achieved, Bock's Army Group B was, after all, no more than the bait for the trap, tempting the enemy to throw a blow toward it and then to grasp his arm.

On that Black Friday, 10 May, as news of the invasions of Holland and Belgium were coming in, further to the south another force was rolling into its battle positions. It was von Rundstedt's Army Group A and it represented the blow to the stomach, the most important part of Operation Scythe-stroke. And heading the reapers was a Panzer Group — virtually a tank army — under von Kleist. Never had such numbers been seen before. As it crossed the frontier that morning it formed a seemingly endless procession which, had its vehicles been placed head-to-tail, would have stretched back some 700 miles, a distance approaching that from New York to Chicago or from London to Madrid.

It was covered by wave upon wave of fighters. Insofar as their role was to guard the advancing columns from the French Air Force, they were redundant. None of its planes took to the skies, notwithstanding the fact that the French military attaché in Berne had warned Gamelin on 1 May of a German blow likely to fall in the Sedan area between the 8th and 10th. There is no evidence that the information was thought worthy of transmission to the armies in the region, Corap's Ninth

and Huntziger's Second, whose point of junction was in the Mézières–Sedan area.

Not even the Whitsun leave· pattern was disturbed, so that thousands of men and officers were dotted in all parts of France. Nor was there much sign of alertness and activity among those still at the front. Over the months of the 'drôle de guerre' vigilance had progressively fallen off. Hours of work, short as they were, were begrudged nonetheless and often evaded. On paper an ambitious plan for fortifications existed and, had they been completed, the German advance would have been considerably impeded. Unfortunately energy was lacking and they were left half-finished even in the most crucial parts of the line.

The Ninth Army held a sector from Namur in Belgium, along the Meuse to Mézières. Its commander, Corap, was a shy, portly man of sixty-two, for whom the sole highlight in an otherwise uneventful military career had been his capture of a Moroccan rebel chieftain in

Above: General (later Field Marshal) Fedor von Bock, whose Army Group B conquered Holland.
Right: Luftwaffe Field Marshal Hugo Sperrle.
Far right: Army Group A's drive to the Meuse: 10–14 May.
Below: German grenadiers and riflemen in northern France.

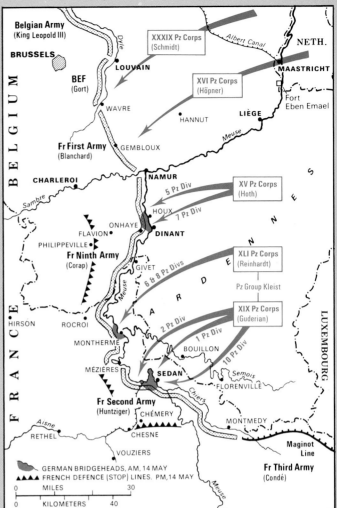

1925. Huntziger, commanding the Second Army, was under sixty, a slightly remote, but highly intelligent soldier, who nearly became Commander in Chief. Corap's troops were, of course, to become involved in the Belgian battle and so weakened. Huntziger had convinced himself that the area east of his line, the Ardennes Forest, was impenetrable, and that much of the sector beyond the Maginot Line was held by Class B reservists, men of thirty and over, bitterly resentful of having been taken away from their shops and businesses, grown fat and flabby on inactivity. Many, indeed, were of that class — the white collar workers — which in Germany had given Hitler such enthusiastic support. Having been through much the same sort of experience as their German counter-

Left: German motorcyclists speed through a village south of Amiens in their rapid drive to the Channel. Below: Wehrmacht troops pass through a northern French village 'softened up' by German bombs. Right: The Wehrmacht's ten-day drive to the sea.

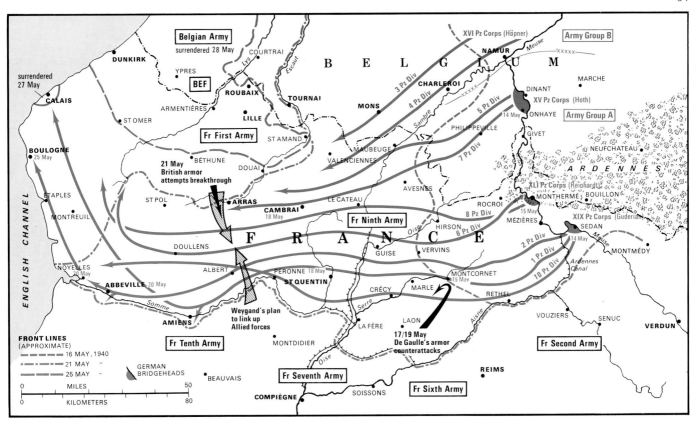

parts – the pressures of economic slump and inflation – they were ready to find the self-same scapegoats in big business and the Jews.

As in Belgium, the first reaction to news of a German approach was one of panic as men on leave tried to get back to their units, clogging roads and railway stations. The scene resembled that of August 1914 when the Germans were advancing on Paris, but this time there were no taxis to the Marne.

The whole situation had, of course, been made more difficult precisely by the invasion of the Low Countries. In order to go to their assistance, the Ninth Army had had to unseat itself from its prepared positions to give continuity of line with those who had moved up to the Dyle.

Only at Gamelin's headquarters in Vincennes was there calm. This might have been welcome had it sprung from confident realism; it was actually that calm which comes from seeing a situation in quite deluded terms. Gamelin issued an Order of the Day on 10 May, ending dramatically with Pétain's words at Verdun, 'Nous les aurons,' a singularly inappropriate and ominous note to strike in view of the disaster that battle had proved and how little the French needed reminding of it. He then ordered the units facing the approaching Panzers to cross the Meuse while cavalry – two brigades of which actually were on horses – was sent out to delay the enemy. He then returned to his maps confident that he would have given himself time to regroup his forces to meet the threat when its shape had become clearer.

The cavalry, as if holding off Kleist's tanks were not enough, was also to act as reconnaissance, gauging the enemy strength, a task which should have been

Below: German motorized battalions pass the outskirts of Sedan near the Meuse.

Left: A captured French Char B tank in northern France.
Right: A French town burns under Luftwaffe and artillery attack prior to its seizure by the Wehrmacht.
Below: PzKw-IIIs and Panzergrenadiers pass swiftly across the rolling countryside of northern France.

done from the air. It found not only that the enemy was much further forward than it had conceived possible, but also that he was present in infinitely greater numbers. In part, this was due to the fact that the Belgians had failed to provide obstacles to armored advance and had even left roadblocks unmanned. By evening one French force had run straight into the spearheads of Guderian's I Panzer Corps. By morning all the cavalry units had had similar experiences. The results were as can be imagined, but sensibly the French forces did not linger to try conclusions. Under fire from the automatic weapons on the German tanks they scattered into the woods.

Later the German generals were able to say that this part of *Sichelschnitt* was less an operation than an approach march, a phrase which sums up their disdain for the resistance they encountered. It was, as Blumentritt said, 'easily brushed aside.'

The 'approach march' through the Ardennes took only some forty-eight hours instead of the nine or ten days Gamelin had been counting on and which would have given him ample time to concentrate his forces on the left bank of the Meuse. Similarities with 1914 were constant and, naturally enough, were much quoted at the time. As then, the French Army was caught unawares by a much stronger one, not because it had not

Above: The ruins of a French town near the Channel coast.

provided itself with the means of fending off the blow, but because of doctrinaire theories of the shape the war would take and an obstinate refusal, in the face of mounting evidence that they were wrong, to alter them.

The delaying cavalry screen which had sallied out from the Meuse had not only failed in its primary task, but also in its secondary one. It had never got close enough to the enemy to assess his strength. Gamelin was as much in the dark as ever as to what was happening. He therefore reverted to the conviction that it was a mere feint and that the real struggle was further north. Although the harsh facts were shortly to force themselves on those in the field, they required a series of ascending steps from division to corps, from corps to army to army group to front before they reached GHQ at Vincennes. By the time they did, Gamelin would already have made his exit.

On 12 May while the Allied forces in the north were experiencing their first devastating taste of the new kind of war in Belgium, the Panzers leading Rundstedt's thrust were through the forest. That day Guderian's Corps took Bouillon

Left: Messerschmitt Bf-110 C-1 bombers on a French airfield.

Right: General Heinz Guderian checks a road map for directions in the drive across France.

just inside the Belgian side of the Franco–Belgian border, and then began swarming across the border itself in the direction of Sedan which lay on the east bank of the Meuse.

Few French cities, indeed few in Europe, can have had quite so calamitous a history as this one. It was at Sedan in 1870 that the troops of Napoleon III, egged on by the pretty, empty-pated Empress Eugenie, met the Prussians to recoil defeated, leaving the road to Paris open. In 1914 it fell within the first weeks of the war and remained in occupation thereafter until the Armistice. Now, once more, it was to be associated in the French mind with defeat and humiliation.

From Gamelin went the order to hold the city at all costs — though there was only the cavalry who had fallen back there to do so. The seriousness of the situation did not seem to have registered. He had convinced himself that the enemy would have to assemble before Sedan and would need something like a week. In fact, by the afternoon of that Whit Sunday, 12 May, Guderian's tanks had reached the Meuse on either side of the town. By 1900 hours they were deployed along the east bank as far as Dinant. The defense of Sedan was outflanked and the cavalry had to retire across the river, blowing up the bridges. As in 1870 and in 1914, the Germans were in Sedan, this time unopposed.

Even now the confidence of French command was unshaken finding justification, no doubt, in one small success. The Air Force had taken to the skies that day and in repeated sorties had brought down thirty of the enemy without loss. When the two sides met the French could tell themselves there was no doubt who was superior.

Of course a crossing of the Meuse by the enemy would bring him into France proper, the river being a far more real frontier than the nominal one north of Sedan. He had a major disadvantage: he had to cross. The river was sixty yards wide and without fords. On the French side there was excellent observation from the Marfée Heights and some 140 guns had been massed along it. Before a crossing could be attempted, the enemy would have to bring up his own artillery. The French remembered the great Skoda guns of 1914, lent to Germany by its Austrian ally, so utterly devastating in their effect but so cumbersome to move, and they imagined something similar would be attempted now. Time, as the well-worn catchphrase ran, was on the Allies' side. So much so that there were

Right: The ruins of Calais after the German occupation.

already those thinking offensively about a counterattack across the river to retake Sedan.

During that Whit Sunday Schmundt, Hitler's personal aide-de-camp (ADC), had asked Kleist what his intentions were: would he wait to concentrate his troops so that he had his main body of infantry in support, or would he go for a river crossing right away? The question reflected the growing apprehension at OKW. Pictures taken by air reconnaissance had been processed and showed that the Meuse line was far better defended and possessed a greater number of fortifications than had been supposed. It was not until later that a further examination by experts showed their true, half-finished state. Though Kleist did not know this at the time, he told Schmundt that he proposed to attack at once, catching the French before they could draw breath, but insisted that to do so he expected the full support of the Luftwaffe to make good his own lack of artillery. This Schmundt promised and Hitler was as good as his word.

Before going to bed himself, Kleist issued his orders for the crossings to begin at 1600 hours the next day for the purpose of establishing bridgeheads. The main blow would be delivered by Guderian's corps.

Early on Whit Monday French reconnaissance reported German forces, including motorcyclists, tanks and infantry, emerging from the cover of the Ardennes and making for the river. Once targets had been registered, the French artillery opened up on what was the gunner's ideal target — thickly concentrated masses of the enemy. But they were hampered from wreaking the destruction they might have done by two factors. The Meuse at that point runs through a gorge with steeply wooded banks running down to the water making direct observation impossible. The other was that they were short of ammunition. The German casualties were relatively high, although not so high as to persuade them to revise their intentions.

Since there was no reply from German artillery, the defenders could hope that the attackers had been caught off balance. By midday these hopes were dashed. Holding strict formation until one after another they peeled off to dive, the Stukas came and continued to come for the next five hours. Kleist, in his orders, had rashly promised that almost the whole German Air Force would be supporting his advance and so it must have seemed to both attackers and attacked. In all, there was something like a thousand planes in the air and, at the same time, there was little sight of the French Air Force. Those aircraft which did appear fell quick victim to the Messerschmitt-109s waiting to pounce.

AVIS
aux
Militaires FRANÇAIS

Les militaires français isolés
s'adresser, tant pour le ravitaillement
que pour le regroupement,

au CINEMA FAMILIA,
Place de la Nation

et la Caserne des Gardes Mobiles
près de la Citadelle

Calais, le 23 Mai 1910

Le Maire,
A. GERSCHEL
Vu le Commandant d'Armes,
De LAMBERTYE.

AVIS aux
Militaires Britanniques

Les militaires britanniques isolés doivent
être dirigés, tant pour le ravitaillement
que pour le regroupement,

a l'Usine DUCHÊNE
rue du Pont-Lottin, (coin rue des Communes)

Le Maire A. GERSCHEL
Vu le Commandant d'Armes
De LAMBERTYE.

NOTICE for the
BRITISH SOLDIERS

The alone british soldiers must be directed,
as well for the nourishment as for the regroupement (reassemblement) towards

"USINE DUCHENE"
Pont-Lottin Street "corner Communes Street"

The Mayor, A. GERSCHEL
Vu le Commandant d'Armes
De LAMBERTYE.

AVIS
à la
POPULATION

Par ordre de l'autorité militaire
Toute Circulation
entre l'intérieur et l'extérieur
de la Ville
est INTERROMPUE

Des officiers et détachements français feront
la police de la Ville et interdiront tout stationne-
ment sur la voie publique.

Calais, le 23 Mai 1910

Le Commandant d'Armes,
de la Place de Calais,
De LAMBERTYE.

Above left: The ruins of a French coastal town.
Left: Transport and light artillery.
Above: Notices diverting traffic in Calais as the pocket closes.

Below: German truck passes French tank traps which have been pushed aside.

Left: German rubber rafts brought thousands of soldiers across the Meuse.

Left: German rubber rafts brought thousands of soldiers across the Meuse.

The effect was as horrifying here as elsewhere. All soldierly reflexes abandoned, the French Class B reservists threw themselves on the ground and into pillboxes, arms clasped over heads to try somehow to shut out the dreadful tumult. There was adequate anti-aircraft artillery and it could have slaughtered the attackers. The crews dared not expose themselves in the open to man their weapons.

Then at exactly 1600 hours, with the earth still falling in showers from the bomb explosions, the German shock troops began falling into their inflatable dinghies, four at a time, paddling themselves across the river and leaping out as they reached the far bank, to dodge from cover to cover as they ran toward the French pillboxes. There had been some anxiety about attacking without formal artillery preparation; now they discovered the Stukas had done the work more effectively than shells ever could. It was true that as a strike weapon the dive bomber was haphazard, but it more than made up for this by its psychological effect. Soon after, Kleist's guns did open fire, compensating in accuracy for what they lacked in numbers, using antitank and anti-aircraft guns in a formal artillery role to silence the French pillboxes. Guderian, who crossed over in the first waves while the enemy bank was still under fire, found the troops overflowing with confidence, now convinced that the battle was theirs. Late that afternoon he ordered the tanks loaded on rafts to be ferried across the river.

In contrast the French were in a state of shocked, half-hysterical collapse. Only in a few places was there any attempt at resistance. The commander of one unit, the 55th Division not yet involved, was just contemplating how best to undertake the counterattack he had been ordered to make when his command post was overrun by *poilus*, rushing from the scene of the battle, in trucks or on foot, chattering and shouting dementedly, many without their weapons, while many of those who had them were firing them off 'like madmen,' in the general's words.

There was, to be sure, a second defense line behind the Marfée Heights, but it had been located so close to the first that it fell in the same stroke.

By nightfall Guderian's Panzers held the heights and both lines. In one place, because of the lack of artillery support, the 10th Panzer Division had had a difficult time crossing the river, but had managed it all the same. Elsewhere an infantry unit, the 1st Rifle Regiment, had pushed forward some six miles and was in

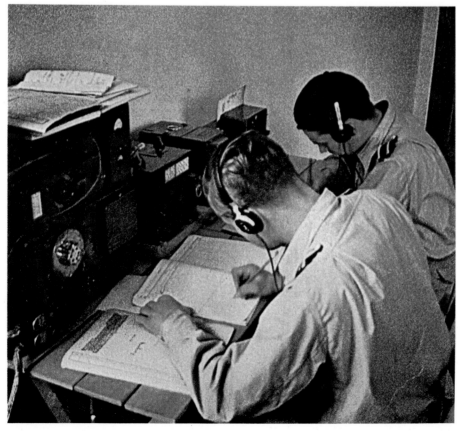

Left: Luftwaffe radio operators at work.

Right: Three stages of an attack by two Ju-87 Stuka dive bombers.

Chéhery. The German lodgment on the west bank of the Meuse was three miles wide and varied between four and six miles in depth. German army engineers worked through the night to build pontoon bridges so that the armor could pour over. Sedan was now part of a dangerous salient taking in the river itself and jutting into the French defenses.

However, results everywhere had not been so favorable to the attackers. About fifteen miles north of Guderian's bridgehead was the XLI Panzer Corps under Reinhardt, charged with seizing a bridgehead across the river at Monthermé between Sedan and Dinant. Here the Luftwaffe had failed to play its promised role and the only cover for the infantry assault was from the guns of the tanks. The crossing was made, nonetheless, but the troops were held down by a tenacious defense mounted by the French 102nd Division and the struggle remained deadlocked.

Just below Dinant, too, there had been setbacks. Here the 8th Panzer Division was to have crossed the river which at this point twists and turns through thickly wooded and rocky gorges. In fact units of Corap's Ninth Army had advanced and made full use of the advantages of terrain available to it by taking up positions among the rocks where even heavy guns could be concealed. It happened, however, that the 8th Division was under the command of a forty-eight-year-old German General Erwin Rommel. Typically he decided to see how things stood for himself and discovered the accurate French fire was destroying the assault boats as they were launched.

It must be said, however, that the subsequent French disaster was due far more to their own negligence than to Rommel's personal intervention. At one point along the river, motorcycle units had discovered a weir left intact by the demolition squads and, since it was wide enough, they drove straight over it. Their temerity was reward by withering fire from the French 66th Regiment lying in wait. Just after this first skirmish, successful from the French point of view, the regiment was relieved but the relieving force, instead of occupying the 66th's positions, actually took up a line well to their rear and so out of range of the weir. In these circumstances the German motorcyclists crossed freely, dug in and held off French attacks all through the 13th until reinforcements sent by Rommel were able to come to their aid.

The lodgment was small. In fact it was small enough that a single assault backed with armor would have been enough to

Right: A Ju-52 transport over the French Channel coast.

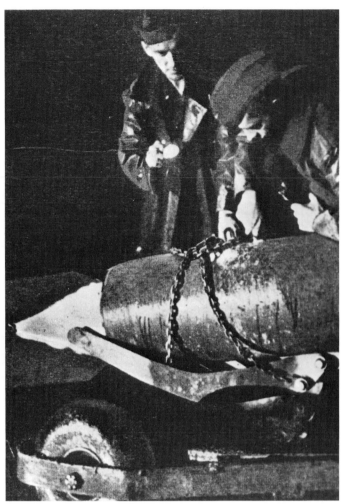

Above: Luftwaffe pilots study their charts before a night raid.

Above: A bomb is checked before it is loaded on a Stuka.

bring about its destruction. Although the Germans awaited it, the only counter-attack was a small raid by tanks and a machine-gun carrier. Through the day it was possible to ferry only fifteen tanks across the river. But it was enough: Rommel's bridgehead was secure.

Yet there was still an opportunity for throwing the enemy back across the river had the French been capable of the effort. Typical of their response was the fate of the counterattack at Dinant. Their 1st Armored Division had been railed to Charleroi on the 12th for this purpose. Its progress was delayed by refugees and a shortage of gasoline. Then it was decided to await the arrival of a French colonial division, the 4th North African, before attacking. By the time all was ready it was too late. Rommel's tanks were breaking loose. Within a short time he was at Onhaye and four miles west of the river.

An early morning attack by two French infantry regiments along Guderian's front was no more fortunate. Their action was postponed for six hours because not all the forces had been assembled and it was not until 0830 hours that they began to advance. Had they moved earlier, even in weaker formations, at the scheduled time, they would have tipped Guderian's forces back into the river. As it was, the Panzers had so grown in numbers that they too were breaking out of their lodgment and caught the French tanks on their flank. Half of them were destroyed with no visible effect on the enemy.

In an effort to make up for the Army's failure to stop the German crossing, 200 aircraft, forming a combined Allied attack group, bombed and strafed the German pontoons throughout the day. The cost was exorbitant – the British alone lost thirty-five planes – and it produced no real dislocation of the enemy movement. In fact, the gap in the French line was actually prised wider during that day.

Yet another opportunity was now to present itself but the defenders were in no better position to take advantage of it. Having crossed the river, the 1st and 2nd Panzer Divisions were ordered to swing

Left: Wehrmacht troops abandon their rubber boats after crossing the Meuse.

west, which actually brought them around ninety degrees to cross the Ardennes Canal and by this maneuver reach around the flank of Corap's Ninth Army.

In so doing they were, of course, exposing their own left flank to Huntziger's Second Army which had just received its first strategic reserve. The 3rd Armored Division was an elite unit, filled with contempt for the way the Meuse defenders had turned their backs on the enemy and determined that they were going to do better. Orders arrived late; again there were fuel shortages and by the time they were ready the chance had once more eluded them. All they could do now was take up static positions with their tanks dispersed over a wide front.

Huntziger was left with no alternative to withdrawal, increasing yet again the gap between his own and Corap's forces. At the same time he faced a dilemma as to which direction to take. He could either open up the Maginot flank by moving northward or leave open the approaches to Paris by going south. Unable to make a decision without some guidance about the strategic intentions of his superiors, he turned to them for it, ascending one by one the tiers of the command system. And one by one they denied him what he sought. At the top he was told to do the best he could! The fact was no one knew where the Germans were heading. Huntziger opted for a movement back upon the Maginot Line and by so doing separated himself from Corap by some ten miles.

Corap was having his own problems. With Guderian round his flank, he was also under remorseless air attack and had had his headquarters smashed and his communications cut. Even his cavalry had suffered without raising a lance in anger as Messerschmitt-109s, flying unhindered

at low level, machine-gunned their hapless horses.

Faced with an additional threat as the enemy forces in the Dinant pocket grew in strength he decided on the 15th to pull back from the entire Meuse line. He sought and received Billotte's approval for a withdrawal to supposedly prepared positions along the Belgian frontier on a line running from Rocroi to Signy l'Abbaye. The intention was for him to concentrate here and deliver the fatal counterstroke. When they reached the line, his men found it was scarcely more than a fiction. It contained the elements of fortifications in the form of pillboxes and similar structures, but was unmanned. Indeed it was so totally unmanned that when the infantry of XI Corps arrived to take up their new positions they actually found the pillboxes locked up and had some difficulty in finding the engineers who had the keys! Thus there was the quite ludicrous situation of troops locked out of their own defenses.

Above: A Wehrmacht sniper takes aim in a northern French town.

Looked at overall, the picture that presents itself is that of the commanders of two adjacent French armies, facing a common crisis, each reacting according to his own assessments with no one able to conform to a general plan. The result was to offer the enemy just precisely what he, of all conceivable enemies, was in the best position to take the advantage of: a great corridor down which he could steer his tanks. This was a moment in which the Battle of France was lost.

Guderian's tanks were pushing Corap northward, while Rommel's were sweeping out of the Dinant bridgehead like ants from a disturbed nest. With two of history's most brilliant armored commanders facing them, the chances for the defenders now looked decidedly un-

Below: A Belgian soldier surrenders in a Flemish coastal town.

Below: German poster in occupied Verdun warns civilians that looting may be punishable by death.

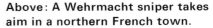

APPEL

à la POPULATION

Malgré les affiches apposées sur la plupart des magasins par l'autorité allemande, celle-ci se rend compte que le pillage et le vol continuent même dans les maisons particulières.

Le Maire de VERDUN a le devoir de rappeler à la population qu'un tel délit est passible de **peines très sévères** pouvant aller jusqu'à la **CONDAMNATION A MORT.** Il dégage toute responsabilité si les patrouilles allemandes étaient appelées à faire usage de leurs armes sur les délinquants.

Il est **interdit** de pénétrer pour quelque motif que ce soit dans les maisons non habitées sans un ordre signé du Maire ou sans être accompagné d'un agent de police.

VERDUN, le 2 Août 1940.

Le Maire : CONÉ

Imp. R. MARCHAL — VERDUN

promising. The Franco-Belgian frontier line was, of course, Corap's position for stopping Guderian. What it overlooked was another threat. Rommel's Dinant bridgehead was actually behind the Ninth's shoulder and to make matters worse, anxious to reach the coast by the shortest possible route, he had set as his forces' first objective a point eight miles beyond Philippeville, which was itself along Corap's line. The French general had stationed himself in exactly the position to be stabbed in the back.

At Philippeville the 1st Armored Division was making preparations for its counterattack so that its tanks were static, having just been refuelled. Since, however, the divisional commander was realistic enough to believe that withdrawal was more likely to be their lot, he had of his own volition sent his guns and other ancillaries to the rear. It was, accordingly, the parked guns which Rommel's force, with he himself in the

Above: General Heinz Guderian leaves his headquarters.
Below: The Focke-Wulf-200 Condor bomber which was originally designed as a commercial airliner for Lufthansa.

lead tank, first encountered. Taken entirely by surprise, the frightened crews dived for the cover of the woods as the Panzers opened fire. There was a show of resistance mainly at Flavion, where the French recovered sufficiently from their surprise to fight with accustomed gallantry, destroying an estimated 100 of the enemy tanks.

They were defeated just the same. By the end of the day, the defenders had sacrificed all but seventeen of their own tanks. In this, the first tank battle of the war, the French had been worsted.

The usual Stuka strafing had preceded the tank attack and the worst sufferers from this had, naturally, been the infantry and other support units. As Rommel's Panzers burst through they found themselves in the midst of broken, demoralized men. All ranks, from highest to lowest, began giving themselves up.

The Germans had broken out of two of their three bridgeheads, but in the third, at Monthermé, Reinhardt's XLI Panzer Corps had been held by a determined defense for three days. Here at least the Stukas had not totally demoralized their opponents, though much of the rear transport had been destroyed. However, on the 15th Corap ordered them back to his own frontier line. It was at this point that the cohesion of the defense broke. Pursued by the German tanks, taking full advantage of the chance now offered to break out of the constriction of the bridgehead, the withdrawal degenerated into a rout. By evening Reinhardt had advanced thirty-seven miles from the Meuse to Montcornet. He was only eleven miles from Ninth Army headquarters at Vervins. That same evening Giraud took over command of the fast disintegrating Ninth Army. A brokenhearted Corap, relieved of command, left his headquarters for the last time.

Above: The Ju-52 transport was called _Tante_ or 'Auntie' by German soldiers who were carried to fields of action in France.

The entire German forces were out in the open, but the toll in sheer fatigue had been enormous. The men were bleary-eyed from exhaustion. Nevertheless there was a general unwillingness to abandon this opportunity to make hay in the French sunshine. When Kleist ordered a halt on the 15th, instead of welcoming the rest, Guderian protested vehemently and was actually granted a twenty-four hour reprieve. His men, as he was afterward to write, had gained a second wind from the realization of the magnitude of the victory they had won and of the opening it gave them. The members of tank units, separated during the battle of the Meuse bridgeheads, began to come together and shouted congratulations to one another across open hatches. There was little sign of the defending forces and when, here or there, some small body of them appeared they invariably gave themselves up. Often they would be found crouching in ditches among civilian refugees.

By nightfall on the 16th Guderian had advanced fifty-five miles from Sedan. His twenty-four hours of grace was now up, but he did not intend to abandon pursuit 'until the last drop of gasoline.' On the 17th, however, he was summoned before Kleist and testily reminded of the halt order of the 15th. This was to be put into action right away.

Guderian lost his temper and threatened to resign on the spot. The situation was saved only by the intercession of List, the Twelfth Army commander, and as a consequence Guderian was told that while he must halt, he could if he wished carry out reconnaissance in force. Of this concession he made the fullest use, though he still felt a restraining hand had been placed upon him.

The reason for Kleist's action in halting Guderian was by no means purely out of consideration for the physical state of the troops. It could well be said that if fatigue was all a soldier suffered in modern war he was uncommonly lucky. Kleist was, in fact, no more than the mouthpiece of instruction from OKW which had been seized by a sudden panic. War was not like this. It had all been too easy — too good to be true. Not even Hitler, at root the instigator of it all, was

**Above left: Air traffic controllers on a German forward base.
Above: Kriegsmarine and Luftwaffe officers plan their next moves.
Right: Wehrmacht artillery is moved forward under the eye of a PK (Propaganda Company) camera.**

free from doubt. He knew the French were liberally supplied with armor and that on equal terms theirs was superior, and he was nervous because of reports over the past twenty-four hours that it was growing increasingly active. The assumption could only be that his troops were moving into the main enemy concentrations.

The truth was that the French armor had almost ceased to exist. All that remained were scratch forces of miscellaneous vehicles with drivers who had been insufficiently trained and gunners who had never fired their weapons in combat. Nevertheless of these there were few enough. On 11 May Charles de Gaulle had been summoned to the presence of General Georges and put in charge of the 4th Armored Division. Georges told him that since he had so long been agitating for the implementation of the ideas the Germans were now putting into practice, he would no doubt be grateful to have this opportunity himself. The colonel made up his mind to strike toward Montcornet on the 17th, concentrating whatever forces reached him for the purpose. What he got were three battalions to face the German divisions. He pushed forward regardless under the agonizing assault of the Stukas. Guderian's forces simply pushed him aside and did not deem the incident worthy of reporting to Kleist.

Up to now, GHQ at Vincennes had managed to keep the painful truth from the politicians in Paris. Here, as in so much else, Gamelin seemed to be emulating Joffre, who in 1914 had divided France into the Zone of the Interior where the politicians ruled and the Zone of the

Right: French troops captured in Lille turn in their weapons to the Wehrmacht.

Armies where he himself was dictator. Thus he was able to give the politicians only such tidbits of information as he chose. But with the speed of catastrophe in May 1940, the truth could hardly be long hidden and as the situation emerged shock waves reverberated through the capital.

In fairness to Gamelin, he was not acting entirely out of a Joffre-esque capriciousness. It was only after he had been to Georges's headquarters at La Ferté-sous-Jouarre on the 13th — the day the Panzers were crossing the Meuse — that he had learned the true position. The discovery did not, however, prevent his reporting to the French commands overseas on the 15th that the enemy activity was 'lessening in intensity' and that the French front along the Meuse, admittedly 'shaken,' was now 'gradually pulling itself together.' It is hard to know

Above: General von Manstein studies his next move in the Battle of France.

what he would have regarded as an increase in the intensity of enemy activity, since that day the Panzers had broken out of all their bridgeheads and were set to roll back Corap's forces on one front and to reach the coast on the other.

Despite repeated visits by Gamelin to Georges's HQ thereafter, neither general could reach a clear idea of German strategic intentions. Hence neither could make even the first moves in a counter-stroke to it. All they could think of was 'containment' and restoring 'continuity of line.' It was like trying to stop a burst dam by running around with sandbags. By

the time orders had reached the point where one sandbag was to be placed, there were ten more breaches. Often the first breach had grown too big anyway. Left where it was the sandbag sometimes split, sometimes turned into a sorry wet lump, a tiny, futile island in the surrounding flood. All the time the supply of sandbags was diminishing.

On the 15th reports of the state of Ninth Army began to come in from head-quarters' eyewitnesses. They bore evidence of commanders who had no idea where their own forces were, of roads choked with refugees, of troops routed, broken, exhausted — men for whom, their military souls now lost, a uniform was simply a carapace. Even at headquarters it was no better. At La Ferté command had already cracked.

It was only then that Gamelin tele-phoned Daladier, the War Minister. The American ambassador, Bullitt, who hap-pened to be present, overheard the conversation and saw Daladier's eyes dilate with horror. 'You must attack at once,' he shouted down the telephone. 'With what?' was Gamelin's laconic answer. The sandbags had gone.

The terrible effects of the Stukas, already so long known to the men at the front, were understood by the dark-suited men in Paris. If the dive bombing could be stopped, if only the appearance that it was going to be stopped could be given, then a stop might be put to the rot of demoralization which sent seasoned sol-diers to cower for their lives only to reappear when they could hand them-selves over to the enemy. With their own Air Force spread, like their tanks, all over

France and destroyed because it never went into battle in sufficient numbers, the only chance was to appeal to Britain. Churchill promised to do all he could but had to point out that Britain had herself to defend as well.

The 15th had also brought the depress-ing news of the Dutch capitulation with a Belgian collapse imminent, and next day Gamelin ordered a complete withdrawal, the decision being reinforced by accounts of yet greater numbers of men fleeing from the Ninth Army and arriving as far south as Amiens.

In Paris Reynaud decided to move the government to Tours explaining in a telegram to Churchill that Huntziger's retreat had laid open the road to Paris. He finished with an appeal for troops and aircraft. At the same time, he sent for Pétain and Weygand.

In Britain, it must be said, there was considerably less complacency than across the Channel, a product perhaps of the inherited suspicion of the French. It was always seen that since the Maginot Line was crucial to French conduct of the war (it was indeed the entire basis of their war-planning), its outflanking would be

Right: Messerschmitt Bf-110 bomber squadron over France.
Below: Thousands of civilians pour down French roads thereby stopping reinforcements from advancing.
Below right: Luftwaffe bombers pulverized the French Air Force as well as many civilian targets.
Below far right: Me-110 and crew members before a flight.

Above: French troops march down the long road into captivity. Many were released a few months after the capitulation, but others were held as effective hostages by the Nazis.
Left: Luftwaffe air traffic controllers signal another successful strike against French targets.
Below: A PzKw-1 and other transport bivouac in a French field in preparation for a further offensive.

catastrophic. Churchill decided to take a plane at once and go to Paris. Here at a late afternoon meeting at the Quai d'Orsay attended by Reynaud, Daladier and Gamelin, the British Prime Minister could see through the window government officials trundling wheelbarrows of papers to great bonfires in preparation for the move to Tours.

This was perhaps the least depressing aspect of that conference in which the French Commander in Chief explained the precise seriousness of the position. Finally, in his own idiosyncratic French, Churchill asked Gamelin where the French strategic reserve was. Gamelin's reply was a shrug. There was none, he said, *'Aucune.'* Churchill re-echoed in amazement. 'What,' he asks in his own account, 'were we to think of the great French Army and its highest chiefs?'

That very day Rommel's forces advanced another fifty miles. The northern extension of the Maginot Line was broken through after a token struggle in which his own casualties were ninety-four, including thirty-five killed. They took a 100 tanks and 10,000 prisoners. By the following day they were at Laon, less than sixty miles from Paris. In both France and Britain people tried to find

comfort by remembering World War I when the enemy had come even nearer to the city before being repelled in the Battle of the Marne which ended the great German advances. But others believed it would fall and in doing so break the heart of French resistance. On the 18th Guderian was advancing once more and had captured St Quentin and Peronne. To his north Rommel reached the scene of the world's first tank battle, Cambrai.

In view of the mounting threat to Paris, Georges had appointed Giraud to command a special covering force. Even to reach his new headquarters at Le Catelet required a circuitous journey. When on the night of 18th he got to it, it was to find the Germans were there before him. He and two officers split up to try to find their way back to the French lines. Early that morning he was picked up by a patrolling German tank and became a prisoner. By the 19th Guderian was across the old Somme battlefield.

Above: Wehrmacht troops break through some barbed wire in a propaganda film.

One of the few French units, still a cohesive and aggressive force, was de Gaulle's 4th Armored Division. On that day they saw an opportunity and attacked the Germans near Laon, despite unceasing assault from the air, penetrating the German line. Even Guderian admits the attack might have provoked a crisis, but in the afternoon de Gaulle was ordered to disengage as his forces were needed more urgently elsewhere.

At Vincennes, it had at last dawned that the German objective was not Paris, but the coast. There was, of course, some relief at this and the planned evacuation of Paris by the government was cancelled for the time being. On the other hand, if the German move succeeded, the armies

in Belgium would be trapped. They must, therefore, extricate themselves. The speed with which the enemy was moving probably meant that his line was comparatively thin, susceptible therefore to determined assault, especially if it came from both sides, from, that is to say, both north and south. This opportunity perceived, it was at once seized upon. The trouble was that it required rapid movement from the three armies in Belgium which were engaged in a struggle for survival against Bock's Army Group B.

Nonetheless on the 19th Gamelin issued the relevant orders, going over Georges's head with his 'Personal and Secret Instruction No. 12.' This proposed that Army Group 1 should employ its

mobile forces in the north against the German rear, the breach being exploited by the motorized infantry which was to follow, while in the south the Second and Sixth Armies were to strike toward the Meuse.

He did not survive to see the plan executed, for on that day he was replaced by Weygand who cancelled these orders at once. In doing so, he was actuated not by any basic opposition to Gamelin's plan. He simply wanted 'to see for himself' first. It was this which sent him off on his difficult flight to Belgium to meet the commanders of the three armies, but it also meant that the opportunity was allowed to slip away. By the time orders were given the armies were

recognized the need to take some kind of counteraction. In fact he was being urged on by Ironside, the Chief of the Imperial General Staff who suggested a thrust to open up the road to Amiens thereby breaking through the German line. This was beyond Gort's resources — or so he felt. On the other hand a thrust in the direction of Arras might hold possibilities and this had originally formed part of the breakout plan. It was to be timed to coincide with attacks by Blanchard and Prioux who were to advance towards Cambrai and try to link up with Army Group 3 which was supposed to attack from the west. Gort, who believed the French generals would never take the initiative, decided to go it alone, though what resulted was hardly more than a raid in force with three infantry battalions and seventy-odd tanks, mostly light, against Rommel's massed Panzers.

For his part, having first been ordered to halt, Rommel began advancing again in the early hours of the 20th. He had encountered a French force which he had

beaten off after infiltrating their communications' line and by the end of the day was in occupation of the heights overlooking Arras.

It was then he was struck by the British. The Germans were completely taken by surprise. They overestimated the size of the attacking force and spoke of hundreds of tanks and supporting infantry. Rommel believed that at least five British divisions were involved.

Alarm at OKH was such that Keitel was dispatched post haste to Rommel's advanced headquarters and there far-reaching new dispositions were worked out, while two German Panzer divisions actually began to pull back toward the frontier! In fact, on the Allied side, the whole thing was over by the next day, for it had never in reality been more than a raid in strength. From now on, however, German activities were marked by a certain caution and Rundstedt was to declare that this was the only time in the entire campaign that he felt really nervous.

This was only a small sector of a long front and elsewhere the advance had been continuing over the past forty-eight hours with Guderian reaching Amiens on the morning of the 20th. Such was his confidence that he even took an hour off to visit the cathedral before continuing

even more heavily engaged while the German line, which was as dangerously thin as Gamelin had supposed, had been reformed. The 19th had been the very day on which the various Panzer groups had consolidated for the final advance to the coast.

Although Gort regarded Weygand's plan for a joint north-south offensive as unrealizable and had not seriously allowed it to interfere with his other plans, he

Below: Hedgehog road blocks are strewn along the route leading from St Omer to Dunkirk.

down the Somme in the direction of Abbeville. All that was now left for an escape route for the armies in Belgium was to join the bulk of the French forces in the small area between Abbeville and the sea which involved crossing the Somme where, in any case, it widened toward its estuary.

Even this was closing. At 2000 hours an advanced battalion of Guderian's 2nd Panzer Division reached the coast at Noyelles. The approach march had begun on 10 May. It was now the 20th. In ten days they had come some 200 miles, sixty-five of them that day alone. At OKW, as he heard the news, Hitler was wild with joy.

The next step was obvious enough. The trapped forces in Belgium — the elite of French and British Armies — must be crushed out of existence and this done, the entire German might would be free to turn on what remained of the French Army. The next advance must be northward up the coast in the direction of Calais — then Dunkirk. Assessing the situation and realizing how the enemy's mind would work, Brooke wrote in his diary that evening that 'only a miracle can save the BEF now.'

Above: British soldier guards property after an air raid on Arras.
Top right: German troops salute a parade of French forces in the capitulation ceremony in Lille.
Right: A German *Spahwagen* pauses in a deserted French town.
Far right: From left to right, Ironside, Churchill, Gamelin, Lord Gort and Georges.
Below: A group of priests and novices evaculate Beauraingville, 23 May 1940.

THE M

The scene at Dunkirk in June 1940.

RACLE

With Bock on one side and now Rundstedt on the other, the BEF and the other armies in the north were, as Gort clearly saw, far from being in a position to play an active role. They were beleaguered and struggling for survival. This was brought home by the fact that on 23 May it became necessary for him to place his troops on half rations because of his supply situation.

Nevertheless Weygand was continuing to pour out his directives and instructions for offensive action and in general behaving as if everything was going according to plan.

Much as the British Commander in Chief desired to play his full part as a faithful ally, there was one overriding consideration. He had to consider the safety of the BEF which represented by far the greater part of Britain's trained and equipped forces. Its loss would not only undermine irreparably the continuation of the struggle in France itself, but, should France fall, Britain's own ability to defend herself.

Although under orders to give such assistance as he could to a French offensive, he was also convinced that the predominant strength for this must come from the south. The northern armies could only stretch out their right hand when relief was within easy reach. Besides, the same supply problems which had forced him to introduce half rations was also affecting the provision of ammunition. As he told London, he did not have enough to embark on any large-scale ventures. He was becoming increasingly skeptical about any initiatives at all

coming from the south or for that matter from any French force. In these circumstances, he was coming around to the view that perhaps loyalty to his own troops took pride of place over that to an ally.

In practical terms this meant the BEF's withdrawal from the struggle in the north by its evacuation by sea. The French would naturally be invited to participate, but even if they refused the time for unilateral action might come. Plans for this eventuality had been made by both Gort's staff and by the Admiralty. On 20 May a meeting of senior Naval officers took place at Dover Castle with Vice-Admiral Bertram Ramsay, Flag Officer in

charge of the crucial Dover area, presiding. He knew the Channel waters well, having fought upon them in World War I. Now fifty-seven, he had been retired in 1938 and was recalled when the war got under way to become, though none then knew it, the driving force behind the

Above: HMS *Wakeful* on a rescue
mission to Dunkirk. She was
torpedoed the same day as this
picture was taken, 29 May 1940.
Right: Closing the Dunkirk pocket.
Below: Royal Ulster Rifles dig in
near Furnes.

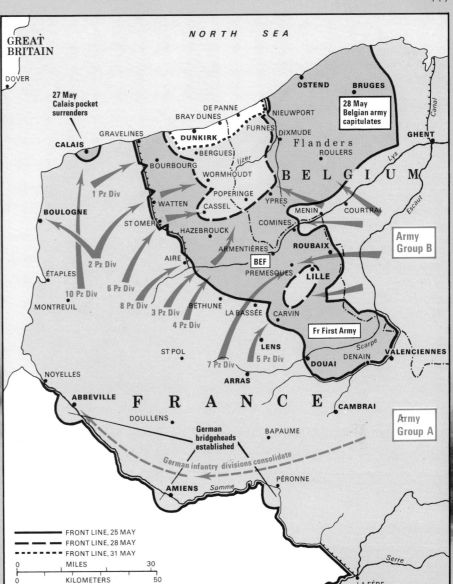

GREAT
BRITAIN

NORTH SEA

DOVER

27 May
Calais pocket
surrenders

OSTEND   BRUGES

DE PANNE   NIEUWPORT   28 May
BRAY DUNES   Belgian army
                  FURNES   capitulates
GRAVELINES   DUNKIRK
CALAIS   BERGUES   DIXMUDE   GHENT
                                                 Flanders
             BOURBOURG   WORMHOUDT   Ilzer   ROULERS
                                                          Lys
BOULOGNE   POPERINGE   B E L G I U M
        1 Pz Div   WATTEN   CASSEL   YPRES
                                            MENIN   COURTRAI
                  ST OMER   COMINES   Escaut
                    HAZEBROUCK
        2 Pz Div   ARMENTIÈRES   ROUBAIX   Army
                          BEF   Group B
        6 Pz Div   AIRE   PREMESQUES LILLE
ÉTAPLES 10 Pz Div
                   8 Pz Div   BÉTHUNE
MONTREUIL   3 Pz Div   LA BASSÉE   CARVIN   Fr First Army
                   4 Pz Div
                                              Scarpe
                         ST POL   LENS   DENAIN VALENCIENNES
                       7 Pz Div 5 Pz Div DOUAI
NOYELLES   ARRAS

ABBEVILLE   F R A N C E   CAMBRAI

        DOULLENS   BAPAUME   Army
German   Group A
bridgeheads
established   German infantry divisions consolidate
                                     PÉRONNE
AMIENS   Somme
                                              Serre
                                   LA FÈRE

——————— FRONT LINE, 25 MAY
– – – – – FRONT LINE, 28 MAY
········· FRONT LINE, 31 MAY

0   MILES   30
0   KILOMETERS   50

118

evacuation of Dunkirk. The name given to this — Operation Dynamo — might well have been a reflection of his temperament. In fact it was chosen because the room in which the meeting took place was one formerly used for an electrical plant and hence known as the 'dynamo room.'

At the meeting it was assumed that not only Dunkirk, but also Calais and Boulogne, would be available for embarkation. Even so the problems were formidable enough. Except for a narrow trench down the middle, the Channel is extremely shallow. This means large vessels could not be used as they could not approach close enough to the coast. Besides, they would be exceptionally vulnerable to fire from the shore batteries and from air attack.

Where were sufficient small craft to come from? The destroyer force was depleted by war and many of the remainder were on patrol duties too vital for them to be spared. The only alternatives were passenger ships. These included the

Above: Guards outside a makeshift POW camp in Calais, 27 May 1940.

DAS BETRETEN DER STADT CALAIS
IST VERBOTEN !

JEDE eigenmächtige REQUISITION
wird kriegsgerichtlich bestraft

DIE KOMMANDANTUR

Above left: A British Cruiser Mk I tank in Calais.
Above: The military commandant of Calais orders that entry into the town is forbidden.
Below: British soldiers surrender in Calais as the pocket closes.

ferries used on the prewar cross-Channel runs. In addition the Dutch had handed over some forty self-propelled coastal barges before their country's capitulation, while, as yet another possibility, a list of paddle-steamers and other pleasure craft had been prepared.

All the same, the forecasts of the Dover Castle conference were hardly encouraging. Even on the assumption that three ports would be open to them, a pickup rate of about 3000 a day was the best that could be hoped for. To evacuate the entire British force, to say nothing of such French and Belgian troops as wanted to get away, would take a very long time indeed and they could scarcely hope for this kind of grace being granted them by the enemy.

A second meeting had taken place at British headquarters in France to decide how best to get the troops to the ships

Left: Due to a low tide British evacuees from Dunkirk were forced to leave by ladder to board HMS *Vanquisher*.

once they arrived. Here, too, calculations were based on the premise that more than one port would be open but daily this was growing less likely as Rundstedt's forces pushed up the coast, threatening Boulogne and Calais. Gort was preoccupied by a more immediate threat: the German breakthrough inside the angle of the L in the Courtrai region. It looked as if the days of Belgian resistance were numbered.

It was this consideration which led him to his irrevocable decision of the night of 25 May when he ordered his 5th and 50th Divisions to transfer from the outer to the inner side of the L's upright. There they could protect his flank as the Belgians fell back and, as must soon

Right: An armada of little boats leave Dunkirk.
Below: Thousands of British and French troops queue up on the Dunkirk beach in their long wait to board an evacuation ship. Some never made it off the beach; others ended up in POW camp.

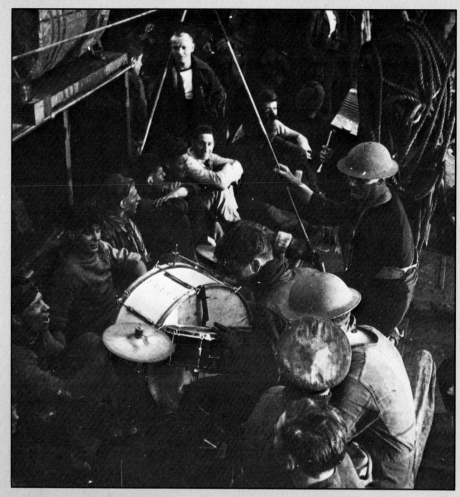

able to say that Gort had ruined the whole thing by his withdrawal of the two divisions. This had so reduced the attackers' strength that the French units who were to have participated had had no option but to drop out. This, in its turn, meant that those from the south would have no one to meet them half way and, lacking sufficient strength on their own, had also had to abandon their endeavor.

Thus the BEF commander became a convenient scapegoat for failure. This version of events was readily accepted by Weygand's countrymen and it was not long indeed before the failure of the entire campaign and the defeat of France was being blamed on the British Commander in Chief. Reynaud asked Major General Sir Edward Spears, the British officer attached to him by Churchill, why it was that in any crisis British commanders always made for the nearest port. He could hardly have touched a more sensitive nerve. He was recalling the events of 1914 when the then BEF, having taken its place in the line, found the French pulling back before the German advance. Their commander, Sir John French, anticipating collapse, decided on a retreat to the coast and was only with difficulty persuaded to abandon it and join in the Battle of the Marne. The British chanced to attack in exactly the spot where there were no enemy forces. Arriving late as they did and unable to believe their luck, the British decided it was a trap and held back allowing the Germans to regroup. Had they acted with more vigor, so the French believed, the whole enemy campaign would have been brought to an end and the war finished before the trench lines came into existence. To be sure, Weygand was later to admit that his own condemnation was premature as Gort was compelled by *force majeure* to take the action he had. He criticized him, nonethe-

happen, give up altogether. Thus the first step toward evacuation was taken. Weygand's offensive looked less and less promising because these two divisions, advancing in the Arras direction, were to have spearheaded the British part of the assault. Weygand, still nursing his dreams of the north-south linkup, was shattered. He begged Gort to reconsider, but found him implacable. He was no less so when Churchill urged him to drive towards Calais where another Anglo-French force was now fighting for its life.

It was very plain that at this point Weygand either believed (there was, of course, Georges's Northeast Front interposed between himself and the fighting troops) or at least pretended to believe that the offensive from the south had begun and was making 'excellent progress.' The exact contrary was the case, since the forces south of the German corridor to the sea were certainly in no position to mount any kind of initiative. However, when it was plain that nothing was actually happening Weygand was

less, for failing to communicate his intentions early enough, a reproach for which there is some justification.

At first under similar criticism from his own government, stung by Reynaud's shafts, the British Commander in Chief was fully vindicated when the War Minister, Anthony Eden, discovered that the offensive in the south was a myth. It was now seen, at least in London, that evacuation was the only course and Eden telegraphed British GHQ to this effect, suggesting they make for the Gravelines' area which was west of Dunkirk and nearer to Calais. The message ended with an exhortation to haste.

Neither Gort nor his staff needed any such urging; above and below Lille, along the upright of the L, his forces were under attack from the German Sixth Army. Strong elements of the same Army were pushing the Belgians back from the crook. On the other southern front there was pressure from a group under General

Opposite: Crew of HMS Vanquisher keep up their spirits after eight days of the Dunkirk shuttle.
Above right: German forces after Dunkirk was taken.
Right: Waiting for a ship.
Below: Packed with evacuees, a trawler leaves Dunkirk for England.

Left: A makeshift pier made up of British lorries viewed quizzically by German troops.

BRITISH EMBARKATION POINTS
FRENCH EMBARKATION POINTS

Hoth and it was quite clear that the intention was to snap the upright off by grasping it between the jaws of a pair of pincers. If this happened, all the troops, French as well as British, below the line running from Ypres to Merville could be cut off from the coast. In compensation, however, everything was now ready for Operation Dynamo to commence and that day orders for it went out.

Actually the planners received timely assistance from two unexpected quarters. On 23 May Guderian's Second Panzer Division began moving on Boulogne and Calais as part of its advance up the coast to annihilate the northern enemy. The French, already there, had been reinforced by British troops sent straight out from England and their combined resistance drew praise from the attackers whose advance was hindered through it. The fall of the two ports naturally had a depressing effect by reducing the number of points of escape, particularly in view of the estimated pickup rate, but it gave Gort three

extra days before he came under full pressure in the Dunkirk area. However, Hitler himself was the person responsible for facilitating the British evacuation, for it was on 24 May that he visited von Rundstedt's advanced headquarters at Charleville. He overrode Brauchitsch's order transferring an army from Army Group A to Army Group B, confirming Rundstedt's order to halt and regroup. By this action the battle was effectively suspended.

Perhaps Hitler had been persuaded by the cautious Rundstedt that his forces needed a *recul pour mieux sauter*. We know that the Führer oscillated between moods of the highest elation when news of fresh successes came in and those of extreme nervousness, as if he believed the whole thing were a vast Anglo-French trap. This might be one explanation, but there are others.

One eagerly taken up in certain quarters has it that Hitler actually wanted to save the British Army. General Blumentritt, Rundstedt's operations' chief, as well as General von Manstein recall that Hitler, to the utter amazement of those round him, sometimes spoke with admiration of the British Empire and of the civilization which the British had brought to the world, and argued the necessity for its continued existence. Certainly there was in Hitler's make-up a streak of pro-British sentiment and there is the growing evidence of his having spent part of his boyhood in Liverpool. Later on in the war, when the Japanese Army was enjoying its great run of victories in Southeast Asia and those around him were openly delighted at the humiliation being heaped on

Right: A Lockheed Hudson leaves the Dunkirk coast as two oil tanks burn.

Britain's Far Eastern empire, Hitler was quick to chide them. If he had had his way, he told them, he would send some of his best divisions to fight on the British side. As Europeans themselves they might grow to regret the power acquired by this yellow race. He believed that once France fell, Britain's position being untenable, she would be forced to make peace and it was his aim to offer one which would be compatible with her honor to accept.

There remains, however, another explanation, one advanced by General Halder. So far the successes of the campaign had been gained by the army and its generals — men of the old school, 'the gentlemen,' so hated by Hitler, who all had a 'von' before their names. Few were members of the party and many shared Hindenburg's contempt for the 'Bohemian corporal.' In contrast with the exclusive band of aristocrats was the Luftwaffe, headed by one of the party's founder members, Reichsmarschall Hermann Göring. Halder suggests that Göring played on his Führer and finally convinced him that Dunkirk could safely be left to the Luftwaffe alone. In this way, the final victory would not be the army's or its generals alone. Hitler and Göring, and hence the party, would share in it.

This certainly accords with the wording of the *Führerbefehl* which speaks specifically of Dunkirk's being 'left to the Luftwaffe.' However, whatever the reasons, we know the effect of Hitler's directive was to bring about a halt of the armies from 24 to 27 May. We know, too, that the officers from OKH down were flabbergasted by it. Said Halder in his diary, 'these orders from the top just make no sense'; Rommel and Guderian reacted similarly.

Through these days the British forces were fighting a delaying action as they moved steadily seawards. Perhaps unfairly, the French had been told nothing of the intention to embark the whole of the BEF, let alone that this had already begun on the 26th. Gort, always straightforward, had wanted to do so, but had been forbidden by Eden. In view of French jibes about British generals making for the nearest port, no doubt the British government wanted to exercise its maximum diplomacy in breaking the news. It was not, in fact, until after the evacuation had started that Blanchard, who had succeeded Billotte as Com-

**Left: Captured French troops at Dunkirk/Many fought valiantly to allow the British to escape.
Right: Some of the thousands of British and French troops captured at Dunkirk.**

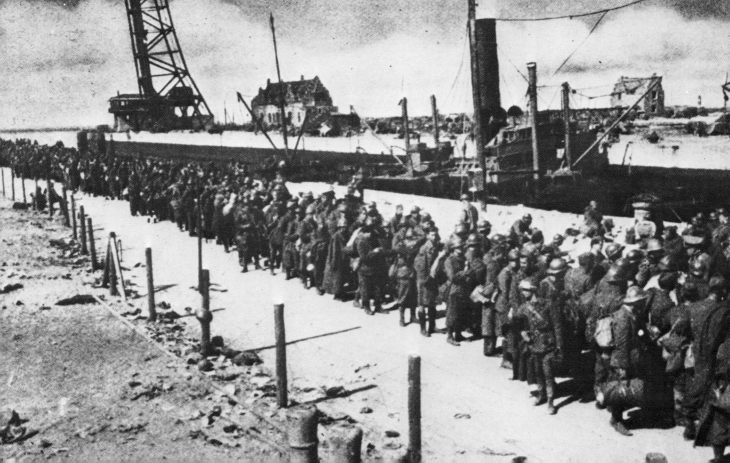

mander of Army Group 1, was told and· pressed to join in.

Up to this time it was believed that the British intended to co-operate in a plan to hold a coastal bridgehead, in Blanchard's words 'with no thought of retreat.' This was to stretch from Gravelines in the west to Nieuport in the east, the defensive line being the canal system running through Furnes and Bergues. Planning was the joint work of the British and French, the representative of the latter being Admiral J C A Abrial who, as *Amiral Nord*, was responsible for the defense of this region.

In amicable co-operation they made their preparations. The area was divided into three and a section allocated to each division. Organization of the defense within the perimeter was entrusted to a British soldier, Brigadier Lawson who, as

soon as all the troops were inside, was to see to the strengthening of the canal defenses to hold off the foe.

The barrier to attack which the canals provided was counterbalanced by the obstacle they formed to the largely mechanized forces as they moved up into it. There was a considerable risk of bottlenecks on bridges leading to severe and dangerous congestion of traffic, and it was therefore decided that most of the transport should be abandoned before these were reached.

There was, naturally enough, the apprehension that this was the final throw in the northern campaign and that there was every likelihood of enemy action wrecking it. At best it was thought that not more than two days' grace would be granted them before the Panzers broke through. In any event it was still believed

in London (and the view was shared by the BEF command) that, on the basis of the original estimate of pickup rate, only about 45,000 men could possibly be saved.

Now resigned to the fact that his counteroffensive was not going to materialize, Weygand began talking of the coming great battle to hold the perimeter whose keynotes would be he declared, 'activity, solidarity, resolution.' When it was finally learned that the intention was not a backs-to-sea struggle but evacuation, the French command was at first aghast, though he later acknowledged the compelling reasons for it and co-operated enthusiastically and loyally. British accounts all too often give the impression that this was entirely one country's endeavor and omit to pay tribute to the contribution made by their ally without which it would certainly not have been possible. In fairness, however, one should add that it had always been the British intention to treat the defenders, French or British, with complete equality.

By the 28th the evacuation was, of course, two days old. What had been achieved in that time had exceeded all expectations. It had only been possible by the meticulous planning of Ramsay and his working party and then by the bravery and determination on the part of those who actually carried it out. Among the technical problems was the size of Dover harbor which was intended to cope with nothing more than cross-Channel traffic. It had only some eight berths and fifty or so buoys. To surmount this the ships had to be berthed in tiers three abreast, while the buoys were used as fuelling and provisioning points.

Outside this unsure haven lay the seaway to Dunkirk with all its hazards. The mines had been swept along the path the vessels would take, but this was only one of the dangers that faced them. There were reports of U-Boats closing in from the North Sea and there was possible German naval action to be feared. Thanks to the admirable co-operation between French and Royal Navies it was possible to maintain constant patrols. It is a savage irony that at least some of those French vessels, so instrumental in the success of the operation, must have been among those which came under fire from the Royal Navy in the Battle of Oran.

The channel down which the ships had to steam might have been mine-free and to a considerable extent free of German naval harassment. There was, however, little protection from the air. The RAF did

Left: Tommies enjoy a darts game waiting for a ship before the pressure grew for ships to England.

its utmost and actually shot down large numbers of the attackers. (The figures given out at the time were 178 enemy aircraft to twenty-nine RAF, but these need to be regarded with skepticism.) The very narrowness of the lane with so much traffic in it made it all the easier to attack and it was described by at least one ship's master as 'hell let loose' as formation after formation of the Stukas swooped to almost mast-level, machine-gunning, flinging up cascades of water from their exploding bombs. To add to this, once the ships approached the French coast they came under fire from the shore batteries. Even those not hit directly advanced under a spray of shrapnel and machine-gun bullets. The toll on the nerves of the seamen, who had no option but to carry out their duties on the open decks, was enormous. In some cases, the master, feeling his men had done enough, asked them if they wished to go on or return. All went on. Many made several such journeys with the attackers growing more venomous each time.

The next problem arose at Dunkirk itself. The city had been exposed to merciless bombardment which had destroyed the harbor works and much of the berthing facilities, drastically reducing the number from which the men could be embarked. Efforts to stop the embarkation increased the destruction and the area was covered in black smoke whose smell lingered rancidly on the ships, while the wrecks of vessels already sunk made navigation difficult. Nonetheless by midnight on Sunday (26 May) 30,000 men had been brought back to Dover, a figure far in excess of that thought possible in the most optimistic forecasts.

It was not only in the Dunkirk roadsteads and around its harbor that the struggle was raging with unprecedented ferocity. The troops were still trying to hold back the enemy forces attacking from all sides of the rapidly diminishing L. On the 27th as Rundstedt's forces went back into action there was pressure all along the southern line with a particularly menacing situation in the area east of Neuve-Chapelle. Here Hoth's Group from the German Fourth Army was in imminent danger of cutting through the upright entirely. It was only by dint of fierce fighting that a narrow corridor was kept open to enable the troops, French and British, to escape coastward.

The failure of their attempts to interdict the movement of the rescue ships to and from Dunkirk on the Sunday made it look as if the Luftwaffe's boasts were to be falsified. What was more, Rundstedt was on the move. Hence there was an order for an intensification of the air attacks on the Monday. More ships were lost. The casualties aboard those which got through mounted and some were forced to turn back by virtue of this alone — they lacked the manpower to operate the vessels.

Through that Monday it became ever clearer that it was no longer feasible to use either the harbor at Dunkirk or the bomb-alley which the narrow, mine-swept channel from Dover had become. An alternative had to be found to avoid excessive casualties.

Thanks to the foresight of the planners, this was available, even if it made the whole enterprise more hazardous. The ships would now have to use a route almost twice as long as the original one. It would run from Ramsgate in Kent to off Ostend and involved negotiating the treacherous Goodwin Sands near the English coast. In an effort to give extra protection as they steamed along it, RAF Fighter Command offered sixteen squadrons of their aircraft to patrol it.

At the same time, with the harbor unusable, the troops would have to be picked up off the beaches. This meant a

Below: Troopships crammed with men disembark in England.

two-stage operation since the larger draft vessels could not risk beaching by coming too close (though some tried and many succeeded), the troops would have to be taken to them in smaller craft. These already stood waiting. Captain Wharton of the Admiralty's Small Vessels Pool had been collecting everything he could lay his hands on for over a week and some forty were moored on the Thames by Westminster. In response to an appeal, still more were on the way, crewed by fishermen, by small pleasure-boat owners who plied off the shores of British seaside resorts, or by weekend yachtsmen. The Dunkirk evacuation moved into its second and most renowned phase.

This armada had yet to reach the beaches, however. In the meantime the only way to get the men off the beaches was by the merchant ships' lowering their lifeboats and the naval ships using cutters and whalers. It was all so slow that only 2500 were taken off during the night.

The position was improved next day after it was decided to use the sole remaining mole of the harbor for as long as possible. This was little more than a wooden walkway on piles, also of wood, through which dangerous currents swept making it extraordinarily difficult for vessels to berth alongside it. That day, however, it was again the military threat which was uppermost in the minds of those commanding in the perimeter. Early on the 28th the Belgian Army surrendered. It had held a line of twenty miles running to the sea and its departure meant that Gort's flank was in midair. The II Corps, under Brooke, already fighting a desperate action against the German Sixth Army had no option but to extend its line to fill the gap. The 50th, 4th and 3rd Divisions were rushed in. Before they could take their place however, the gap was threatened by a German thrust at Nieuport which, had it succeeded, would have brought their troops around behind the evacuation beaches. Luckily the first assault was held by armored cars of the 12th Lancers and while the enemy was regrouping for a further onslaught, the line was reinforced by a scratch force which fought with conspicuous valor, while the French 60th Division and a brigade from the British 4th Division was brought over from the west side.

At the same time, there was a second savage enemy attack on the western side of the line with armored thrusts almost all the way along it. Here as elsewhere the battle was being waged on the British side by almost anyone who could be found. This included engineers, medical orderlies, men returning from leave, physical training instructors and drivers. At one point a chemical warfare unit fought with extreme bravery and tenacity, at another a mobile bath unit and there was even one occasion when a group of chaplains of all denominations took up rifles to hold a bridge at Bergues. The fluidity of the battle meant that communications were frequently lost and all that those in command could do was trust that somehow a line was being held together. Amazingly, this was the case, though often units would be forced back from one point to take up another a few yards further back, managing, nevertheless, to maintain cohesion.

At the bottom of the pocket it was this day that Rommel's 8th Panzers, attacking from one side and Bock's 7th Infantry Division from the other, finally succeeded in cutting off the defenders of Lille at the base of the upright of the L. All that remained there was one corps of the French First Army. Under their commander, General Molinie, they fought on for four more days. Their brave and sacrificial stand drew the highest praise from all quarters, among them their German opponents, who, when they were finally forced to capitulate, accorded them full honors of war. Their action helped their comrades to escape by tying down no fewer than seven German divisions which could otherwise have been employed in investing the perimeter.

There were fierce struggles also going on around Cassel and Poperinge where the defenders were being forced back remorselessly. The following day, the 29th, despite the valor of the defenders, this gradual shrinking of the perimeter went on.

Nevertheless by midnight on that day most of the BEF forces and nearly half the French First Army were within its confines and holding the line of the canal which circumscribed it. When it became clear that the French forces as well as British ones were to be evacuated, Abrial, officially commander in the Dunkirk area, objected. He wanted to retain them for the perimeter's defense still believing he might hold it as a permanent bridgehead. In the end the British command had to contact London and ask them to request Paris to give Abrial direct orders. This done, the embarkation of French troops was allowed to proceed side by side with that of their British comrades now, however, rapidly diminishing in numbers.

At sea the day had been one in which heavy losses were sustained. Two British destroyers were sunk in quick succession, most of the troops aboard being lost with them. A third was sunk later and some six others damaged. By the end of the day the Admiralty was forced with the greatest reluctance to decide it must withdraw all its most up-to-date destroyers from the evacuation fleet since further losses would affect the country's ability to patrol its own sea lanes.

The losses among the passenger vessels were heavy, too. The *Clan MacAlister*, *Fenella*, *Crested Eagle*, *Mona's Queen*, *Polly Johnson*, *Nautilus*, *Normannia* and *Lorina* were among those sunk, set ablaze or so badly damaged as to be useless. None of these vessels' crews could ever have dreamed to what end their craft would come. The *Normannia* for example, had, in peacetime, carried holidaymakers across the Channel. The paddle steamer *Crested Eagle*, like its sister ship *Golden Eagle*, plied down the Thames from London to the seaside resort of Margate.

The mole from which the men had embarked since Monday was now unusable and had to be abandoned so that there remained only the beaches. Now, however, the small craft were arriving. They came in all shapes and sizes: fishing boats, cockle boats, luxury yachts and there was even one man from Littlehampton in Sussex whose tiny rowing dinghy made trip after trip from the shore to the larger vessels waiting in deeper waters. Twenty-five years later he was among those who returned to Dunkirk in a rally organized by a British Sunday newspaper.

As they waited along the beaches, the great snaking queues of men were under almost constant assault from the scream-

Above: Hermann Göring.
Right: The ruins of Calais harbor on
31 May after the Germans seized it.
Below: Dunkirk harbor shortly after
the last ships left. Transport of
every description was left behind.

ing Stukas. On the first days a feeling of terrified helplessness before these attacks in the open had frequently led to panic reaction. Every time a vessel approached the shore, hundreds would wade out to it, a thrown rope would be grabbed by dozens; in many cases men simply walked into the sea and remained floundering in the hope of being seen and picked up. Often the most brutal methods had to be used to ensure that the tiny vessels were not swamped and sunk under the masses struggling to get aboard. Men were pushed off with boat hooks; several masters were forced to draw their re-

volvers. Also men were often seen struggling and drowning as they tried to get to a ship and missed a footing in scrambling aboard or were pushed off to prevent the vessels becoming overloaded.

However, the men soon mastered their fear of their aerial tormentors. They had learned, for example, that their bombing was utterly inaccurate, that the missiles buried themselves deep in the sand and their blast effect was thereby muffled, and that it needed only the most elementary kind of shield, an old mattress, a sheet of corrugated iron, a foxhole, to gain complete protection from them. Where once

they cowered, they now fought back, seizing rifles to take pot shots.

In many cases there was something approaching a parade-ground smartness. The master of one vessel, pulling in, shouted that he could take sixty men. There was no concerted rush. For a moment, in fact, he thought no one was going to answer his summons. Then a sergeant marched a body of men down to the sea and waded in. 'Sixty men, sir,' he said, coming to a brisk salute before turning about himself to return to the remainder, ready presumably to count off the next batch.

Above: The Dunkirk beach after the evacuation.
Above right: Dunkirk harbor, once seething with tension and men, after the German occupation.
Below: Allied transport strewn over the now-quiet Dunkirk beach on 4 June. The last ships had gone.

Humor reasserted itself. 'Any more for the *Skylark?*' masters called out as they brought their vessels into the shallows, just as they had been wont to call out to gather together their parties of holiday-makers for trips around the bay in peace-time. A group of Yorkshiremen began singing, 'Oh, I do like to be beside the seaside.' By the end of the 30th 53,823 men had been landed in Britain that day alone.

On the German side there seemed to be no real idea what was happening. Nor indeed was there any clear plan for the final subjugation of the defenders of the perimeter on the coast, a result the enemy's overwhelming superiority could have brought about with little trouble. They seemed to believe that the forces in the perimeter were in a more or less classical stage of siege, though their communiqués spoke disparagingly of troops trying to get away 'on anything that could float.' It was obvious they had no full appreciation of the scope and success of the evacuation.

Among those who left the next day was Gort. British headquarters, which through its short history had made a succession of moves before the German advance, ended at De Panne on the coast between Nieuport and Dunkirk. One reason for siting it there was that it was at this point that the telephone cable connecting France and Britain entered the sea, making it possible to maintain communications with London from it.

Gort had been instructed to leave once the BEF's forces had been reduced to the size of a corps and hence could be entrusted to a corps commander. This position had now been reached and he had been ordered back. At a final conference of his officers, he appointed Major General Alexander to remain in

command until the last British troops had left France.

Enemy pressure through the day was slowly contracting the perimeter and it was obvious it could not be held for much longer. Intimation of this was therefore communicated to London. This constant pressure on all sides necessitated rushing such forces as could be found to man gaps or to hold a new line a little behind one lost. On the 31st a crisis was rapidly developing around Nieuport, but a fierce assault by RAF Albacores and Blenheims on the concentrating forces from Bock's Army Group B prevented an attack from materializing.

It was on the following day, 1 June, however, that the real danger point was reached. Alexander had told Abrial that he now doubted whether the perimeter could be held until all the men in it were evacuated – most of those remaining now being French.

The evacuation had been going on for a week and, as if to mark the occasion, the Luftwaffe mounted its heaviest raids yet on the city, the beaches and the ships. Simultaneously German army units broke through at two points along the canal line. This compelled a further withdrawal and brought the defending troops to their final line.

To make matters worse, the night was extremely dark so that collisions between vessels and what can only be described as traffic jams along the beaches added to the hazards of war, and the French troops were often unable to understand instructions shouted to them in English. There were also problems of lack of discipline and drunkenness, as had happened during the early days of the British part of the evacuation. In some cases, too, there was downright obstruction – one French officer refused to accept orders issued by British ones of lower rank and revolvers had to be drawn to bring about compliance. For all this 1 June was the most successful day of all as far as numbers picked up was concerned. During that twenty-four hours some 64,429 men were embarked and it was possible to announce that the BEF had been evacuated.

It was the French who had to hold the bridgehead now and who had to fight down to the very beaches, finally to embark themselves. They more than fulfilled their obligations as they had throughout the entire period. But as the enemy closed around the town and the rear-guards struggled to hold them back, a new complication arose. Hidden in cellars, in the shells of half-destroyed buildings and any other place which could conceal them, were French army deserters or stragglers from other units. As they saw a final chance of escape, they too began making their way to the beaches. There was, of course, no way for the beach-masters and men in the craft plying to the

shore to separate the men who had actually been fighting and dying on their country's behalf from those who had shirked the struggle. Thus the numbers awaiting embarkation were well in excess of, perhaps almost double, the anticipated ones. Some 38,226 French troops were evacuated instead of the 30,000 estimated. Undoubtedly this number included many who had allowed others to face the terrors of the battle in their stead. Equally certainly, many of those left behind were among those who had fought with such pristine courage.

On Monday (3 June) the Germans began breaking through into the town itself. Over the next two days they began completely overrunning it. Many prisoners were taken, making a total of 40,000 through the course of the fight for the perimeter. There was besides all the heavy equipment which had to be left behind and much was made of this in German propaganda. Some of it was actually put to use; the Germans were very happy where possible to exchange their own army trucks for the more robust and reliable British-made ones. Later many of them served for transporting the materials used to build the Atlantic Wall which was to keep the Allies out of Europe. British Raleigh and Hercules bicycles, of which large quantities were found, became valued possessions for any who were able to acquire them. German soldiers were seen all over occupied Europe riding them.

Dunkirk was also a graveyard of a more literal kind. The struggle had cost 68,000 British lives and an infinitely greater number of French ones. With ash from the now dying fires and sand blown up from the beaches settling in the creases of their uniforms, they sprawled in the streets where they had fallen, sometimes in such great numbers it was necessary to pick a way over them. This, too, made excellent propaganda for Goebbels.

There was still another casualty – the last vestige of trust that the French held for Britain. Not only did they believe (and still believe) their ally had deserted them in their hour of need, but they also believed he had freely and wantonly sacrificed French lives to do so. This charge cannot be totally refuted. Even while admitting that Gort's assessment was more realistic than Weygand's and that the abandonment of the northern theater was essential, one can still see that from its inception the matter was handled with singular ineptitude, not to say dishonesty, between the British and French governments. Surely, too, it would have been possible to have given at least a show of greater equality in the organization of the operation. The impression given was that it had been the British who got away, and the French who fought and died to allow them to do so. The figures, by themselves, support this: of the

366,000 saved all but 122,000 were British. Of course, this was not the whole story. Dunkirk happened to be the only usable port. It also happened to be in the middle of a British-held sector where, not unnaturally, their troops predominated. Furthermore, the French hesitated before deciding on evacuation. But there were few at the time – or subsequently – who worked out these subtleties, and the bare statistics made of Churchill's claim to Reynaud and Weygand that the troops, British and French, would enter the ships *'bras dessus bras dessous'* another example of British hypocrisy in French eyes.

What particularly stuck in the French craw was what they saw as the blank ingratitude of their ally. Always willing to acknowledge and pay the warmest tribute to the British role in it, the French wondered why the British were unwilling to acknowledge the role of the French Navy or of men like Abrial in the miracle. It was a miracle – the miracle, which in Brooke's words, alone could save the BEF.

There was also another miracle, that which Alistair Horne has pointed out: the effect it had upon the British people. It brought home to them that this was not a 'Phony War.' It was a starkly real one. This realization, far from intimidating them had precisely the effect that, given the history of the nation, might have been anticipated. They prepared for deadly resistance. It was as the Panzers were finally breaking through on 4 June that Churchill struck this chord with his warning to the Germans that, should Britain be invaded, 'we shall fight on the beaches, we shall fight on the landing grounds; we shall fight in the fields and the streets, we shall fight in the hills . . . .'

Later, by September, the fate of Operation Sealion, the intended invasion of Britain was sealed with the Luftwaffe's defeat in the Battle of Britain. German generals like von Manstein were to speculate later about what might have happened had it taken place. They overlooked one factor: more than any other European, the British detested Nazism and that detestation was to be found in every sector of society. There were no crypto-Nazis in the British Parliament; only a few eccentrics saw Hitler as the bastion against Soviet-style Communism. This detestation was infinitely increased by Dunkirk. In the mood of June 1940 an invasion would have been found very bitter and costly for the invader.

THE BATTL

The swastika flies over the Arc de Triomphe after the fall of Paris.

f Dunkirk had engendered bitterness between France and Britain, more followed in the period after the BEF's embarkation. Weygand demanded its immediate return and there is little doubt that the British government was thinking along these lines.

As early as 2 June, Brooke, who had only just got back from Dunkirk himself, was summoned to the War Office to be told to go back to France forthwith to rebuild the BEF with himself as its Commander in Chief. Its nucleus would be those troops still there, numbering some 140,000 and including the men forming token forces in the Saar and on the Maginot Line. They would gradually be increased by troops sent from Britain and from the Dominions.

To Brooke, who expected an early French collapse, the plan certainly did not commend itself on grounds of realism. It would be a very long time before appreciable British forces were available. All the heavy equipment left on the French shore had to be replaced and there were dire shortages of everything down to rifles. The fact was that with notable exceptions, the military bureaucracy in Whitehall had been no more willing than that in Paris to adjust itself to the chilling realization that, unable to cope with the new ways of fighting, the great French Army was about to suffer extinction.

Mercifully there were several other weighty objections to another large-scale

Continental adventure. One was the groundswell of public resistance manifested in the editorial comments in the principal newspapers. Forming part of their argument was the real fear of a German invasion. The Dutch, Belgian and many of the French ports were already in enemy hands. Hitler might well decide that France was a lesser issue and act on his belief that Britain was the true enemy. It was essential that a force sufficient to meet such a threat was retained within her shores.

Above: A wounded and dejected Scottish Highlander after his capture near St Nazaire on the Atlantic coast.
Right: Nazi troops keep firing as the city of Rouen on the lower reaches of the Seine continues to burn in the final stages of the Battle of France.
Below: German motorcyclists speed through another burning village as the final battles for France were being fought.

Above: Mussolini came in for the kill by attacking France on 10 June.

Weygand, on the other hand, insisted that France stood in desperate need of every single soldier who could be sent to her, and given proper assistance could and would continue to resist. This had to be set beside her considerable losses, however. These amounted to some twenty-four divisions, all three of her light mechanized divisions, an armored one and two of light cavalry. He was left with an estimated sixty divisions to face

the Germans' 130, and the French forces were dispersed throughout the country, including some still on the Maginot Line. To bring his full strength against the enemy, a massive regroupment accomplished at top speed would be necessary — and it would still be insufficient.

It was equally plain that Britain was in no position to make good so large a deficit even by denuding her home defenses.

As this harsh truth sank in, the French General Staff was left with two possible answers (though it applied neither). One was to abandon the struggle in France altogether and instead to evacuate the armies so that the fight could be continued from the North African empire. The other was to withdraw to a bridgehead in France itself, a sort of modern Torres Vedras, in Churchill's words, and the Breton peninsula was one which offered itself as a likely place since here

Below: Two French refugees rest their weary feet.
Right: Motorized German artillery stops at the graves of three German soldiers.

it would be possible to maintain contact with Britain across the Channel. It also meant a comparatively short defense line could be held. Insofar as he was prepared to take either plan seriously, Weygand looked more favorably on the second, though he finally rejected it on grounds of lack of time.

Once Weygand knew the British would not return quickly and in strength, he rapidly lost the last vestiges of faith in a successful defense, let alone in a successful end to the war. Those who came in contact with him at this time found his major preoccupation to be the effect on his reputation, hitherto untarnished, of his involvement in a debacle he believed to be of others' making. Like Hitler later, he took refuge in a national heroic myth of his own invention. France, torchbearer of civilization, deserted on all sides, would go down with flags flying, presum-

Right: Panzer division stops to catch its breath near a river in central France.

ably singing the *'Marseillaise'* as the tide of barbarianism lapped ever higher. The playing out of this would take the form of a last, great defensive battle followed by *le deluge.*

Phrases like 'the honor of France' and 'fighting to the death' recurred in communiques and orders and, by their repetition, lost all power to stir. Thus the coming great battle was to be fought along the margins of Somme and Aisne where, in a General Order on 26 May, Weygand directed his forces to take up their positions 'with no thought of withdrawal.' With the awesome responsibility of knowing they would be fighting the battle 'on which the fate of the country depends,' all leaders down to platoon level were to

gird themselves with a 'fierce desire to fight to the death.'

Such injunctions, frequently as they occur in military history, are rarely worth the paper used for their dissemination. The ordinary soldier needs to be exhorted not to stand and die, but to stand and win, and few men face death with the Spartan composure the writers of such missives seem to imagine, especially since they know these writers, safe in their headquarters, are not being called upon to make a similar sacrifice.

What is more, it was exaggerating the gravity of the situation at the very time it needed understating. No one could say France's situation was not serious, but the German forces had not yet achieved

the distance they had in their greatest advances in 1914. Final defeat in war was not measured by the miles an army retires, but by its ability or otherwise to remain in existence.

How far Weygand had gone in accepting that this was the last round is shown by the fact that, no doubt to inspire the one man with the courage to fight on, Paul Reynaud, he told him that should the Army fail, 'I shall have the ghastly job of meeting the Germans, just at Rethondes [where the Armistice was signed] twenty-two years ago, though this time with the roles reversed.'

The front now ran from the coast southwest of the estuary of the Somme upriver to Péronne whereafter it con-

tinued to follow the bank of the river up to the Ailette Canal, then the bank of the Aisne up to Longuyon which represented the beginning of the Maginot Line. It was held by three Army Groups: the 3rd under Besson, the 4th under Huntziger, the 2nd under Pretelat, the command of the last extending to the Maginot Line itself. The front was so long it was held at a density of only one division per seven to nine miles.

Confronting it was an increasingly strong German enemy, freed of all responsibilities elsewhere. Rundstedt's Army had been reinforced by three of Bock's Armies; only his Eighteenth was left in the north where it was mopping up the last resistance in the Dunkirk region.

Left above: An explosion on one of the British ships guarding the entrance to Cherbourg harbor during the evacuation.
Above: British dead on the quayside of St Nazaire.

Below: A Dunkirk-like scene at Cherbourg harbor. Transport of every description was left behind in the rush to get back to England.
Bottom: British trucks block the road leading to St Nazaire to gain a few more precious minutes of time for evacuation.

Troops on a transport ship *Arkforce* wave goodbye to Le Havre as they left the port on 13 June.

Far left: British troops line up on the quayside of a French coastal town prior to their evacuation.
Left: Wounded of the 4th Cameronians arrive at a regimental aid station near Hughenneville.

Altogether ten Panzer divisions were available and these were reorganized into five armored corps of which Bock on the right (and therefore nearest to the coast) received three and Rundstedt on the left, two. The intention was that XV Panzer Corps should break through between the coast and Amiens, the latter already being in German hands, and so into the lower Seine region. The XIV and XVI Panzer Corps were to advance in the general direction of Paris. In a second phase Guderian's Group was to sweep in two parallel columns between the Aisne and Marne in the direction of Langres with the intention of taking the French Armies, by now heavily engaged, in the rear and, at the same time, paralyze the forces in the Maginot Line. It was another case of two Armies — in this case the Panzers — grasping the enemy's arms while a third struck the blow at the solar plexus. For this purpose, the units selected were the Ninth and Second Armies.

However, despite the French deficiencies of manpower in relation to the enemy the odds were not entirely in the

Left: A column of British troops board their ship.
Below: British troops on board head for home.

Germans' favor. The defenders had adopted a highly original device. Instead of attempting the impossible by holding a continuous line, they had constructed a grid of what they called *hérissons* (hedgehogs) arranged on a 'checkerboard' pattern. These were strongpoints, usually well-camouflaged, in houses, woods, villages and anywhere else that could accommodate them. Bristling with weapons including 75-mm guns to be used for antitank purposes, they were, in effect, tiny fortresses which could defend themselves from all sides and even hold out for a time when surrounded.

Though they were to inflict heavy damage upon the attackers, the greatest French armor expert, de Gaulle, was among those who opposed an idea so static. He had rightly divined that the only way to defeat armored assault was by maneuver and actually proposed employing the most modern of the few remaining French tanks, amounting in all to some 1200 vehicles, in two attack groups which could harass the German flanks as their lines began to extend themselves. The idea was dismissed as impractical in view of the time available for formation of the groups. In any case de Gaulle's soldiering days were almost over. On 6 June, now a General, he was appointed deputy Minister of War in Reynaud's Cabinet.

The day before, the battle to decide France's destiny had begun. At five different points along the front held by Army Group 3 which ran from the coast up the Somme Ailette Canal and Aisne to

the confluence of the Suippe, there were withering attacks by the Luftwaffe, the invariable precursor of an offensive. This was not long in coming as the XIV and XVI Panzer Corps began emerging from the direction of Amiens and Péronne. They had no difficulty in crossing the Somme as bridges had been left intact. That day, German radio interrupted its normal transmissions for a special announcement in which Hitler declared that the 'great offensive against France had begun.'

Above: British artillery in action at St Maxent.
Below: British light tanks join the action at the Battle of Quesnoy, 30 May 1940.
Bottom: German prisoners taken by the British arrive at 152nd Brigade HQ at St Maxent.

However, on this occasion the defenders did not quail and flee under the shrieking Stukas. The earlier demoralization of the French forces seemed entirely absent, as the Germans were among the first to realize and admit. Within the hedgehogs the men resisted tenaciously and confidently, inflicting considerable damage on the enemy. Had de Gaulle's mobile 'attack groups' been available at this stage, the entire German advance might have been disrupted and converted into defeat. The basic flaw with the hedgehogs was that, like all fixed forms of defense, unless they could be guaranteed totally to stop or annihilate an enemy, they became useless once the battle had passed beyond them. The defenders in the hedgehogs were cut off, with nothing to deliver the *coup de grâce* to the stricken German tanks, which were able to regroup once they had passed through.

By midday the French assessment of the position was that although their front had been penetrated, the 'hedgehogs' were taking a heavy toll and in several places the German advance had been halted. The question now facing the

French commanders, as Weygand expressed it, was whether the disposition of reserves at these points could have the effect of turning the enemy back. There seemed to be some justification for hoping that it might.

The truth was that, while the 'hedgehogs' had certainly held and the other French forces had fought gallantly, the Germans had secured a wide enough foothold across the Somme to be able to bring up their artillery. Throughout the campaign they had used this with telling effect, while, by contrast, the French, renowned for the devastating barrages in World War I, seemed hardly to respond. Before the attack on 5 June German intelligence reports indicated that their opponents actually had superiority in guns, but, according to Manstein, who

Above: A British light tank moves up to meet the enemy at Quesnoy in late May 1940.

was commanding the XXXVIII Infantry Corps, they remained comparatively inactive and so allowed the enemy to move its own artillery freely. Next day his guns opened fire on the hedgehogs with the result that by that evening, the Tenth Army had to withdraw to a line with its back along the river Bresle and through Hornoy, Poix and Conty. The Seventh and part of the Sixth was forced to withdraw to give conformity, though for the rest of its length the front held.

However, the Germans were now getting the measure of the 'hedgehogs' and on 7 June Rommel, whose 7th Panzers were part of the coastwise

Above: German infantry march through Chatillon-sur-Marne on 12 June.

thrust, were able to push forward quickly simply by keeping to open ground and avoiding them. By the end of the day he was at Forge-les-Eaux. He was now within striking distance of the Seine. A counter-attack failed to affect the issue and, in fact, there was a gap in the defense line with the British 51st Infantry Division and the IX Corps isolated from the main body of Tenth Army. The tide of optimism which two days earlier had been in full flood at French command was now ebbing. The tone of a telephone call from GHQ to the Prime Minister was one of utter depression. The battle had already been lost.

Below: British officers and men study a map in the Somme area as the Allies fell back.

On 8 June de Gaulle, now in the government, visited Weygand at his headquarters. The Commander in Chief told him, 'You see the Germans are passing the Somme. I can't stop them.'

'Right, they're passing the Somme. And then?'

'Then it's the Seine and the Marne.'

'Yes, and then?'

'Then? But it's finished.'

'How is it finished? The world? The empire?'

'The empire? That's nonsense. As for the world, after my fight here, it won't be a week before Britain is negotiating with the Reich!'

As if to give confirmation to Weygand's pessimistic predictions, Rommel next day advanced still further, breaking through a British screen spread on the Béthune and Andelle rivers. Their forces were compelled to withdraw westward to Le Havre, while those on the far side of the gap withdrew southward toward Pontoise, thus increasing the distance between them and making a closing of the breach less possible. By the 9th the Germans were along the line of the Seine at Elbeuf. Paris was once again threatened and hasty defensive measures had to be taken as men from the Paris garrison and from the Seventh Army took up prepared advanced positions from Vernon to Pontoise guarding the westerly approaches.

Meanwhile the government was making ready a second time for its departure from Paris, this time for Bordeaux, where it had been evacuated for a period in the early part of World War I.

Through this period the isolated units of the Tenth Army attempted to hold a small bridgehead between Dieppe and Le Havre in the hope either of reinforcement from Britain or of evacuation. They held out against Rommel's Panzers until finally compelled to surrender on 12 June.

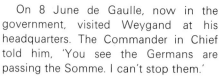

Above: British armored vehicles at Quesnoy on 30 May.
Above right: British troops erect an antitank barrier on the route between Amiens and Rouen.
Right: French soldiers on bicycles move up to defend their territory near the Somme.

Among those taken prisoner was the commanding general of the British 51st Division, General Fortune, whom Rommel personally congratulated on his defense. Later, while the general was in a prisoner-of-war camp, the German general maintained an interest in him.

Savage as the blows were which had already been sustained, the worst was still to come. The focus of the battle shifted to the eastern approaches to Paris. On the 9th Rundstedt's forces joined in the struggle, crossing the Ailette Canal and pushing through Champagne, his strength being augmented by the transfer to him of the XIV and XVI Panzer Corps.

To this fresh development Weygand responded with his usual tinny rhetoric: 'The order remains, for each one, to fight without thought of giving ground, looking straight ahead. . . . We have come to the last quarter of an hour. Stand firm!' The order was, once more, in strict contradiction to de Gaulle's view that in the war now being fought the only proper response was maneuver.

Then came another shock: that day, 10 June, Italy declared war on France. It was an act for which even fervently patriotic Italians felt shame, but Mussolini had long wanted to be involved. As he had remarked to one of his paladins, he needed 'only a few thousand dead' to claim a seat at the peace conference and hence a part in its spoils. Along the Ligurian littoral, down to Nice, was an area of France with strong Italian connections; many of the personal names are Italian and the very name Monte Carlo is

Left: Germans have their boots polished at Château-Thierry on 12 June. They suffered a stunning defeat there in 1918.

witness of the influence of the language. Mussolini, therefore, announced to a massed meeting of his followers in the Piazza Venezia that Italy was about to 'liberate' Savoy, Nice and Corsica. Hitherto he had been restrained by a blunt warning from the American President, Roosevelt, to keep his nose out; not even Hitler had much fancy for him as an ally.

For the unhappy French it was yet another blow on what de Gaulle has called 'the day of agony.' As it happened, however, Rundstedt's arrival had failed to have its anticipated effect. He was forced to seize the Aisne crossings by infantry assault alone in order to obtain bridgeheads for his tanks and most of the attacks had been held. He was able to establish a small lodgment at Château-Porcien, although this, in the French view, was too small to be put to real use. The French had mistaken their man once more. It was Guderian's Corps which had reached Château-Porcien and he pushed the tanks of his 1st Division through the small opening with such speed and vigor that they were soon approach-

Above right: Motorized German units in the Champagne area.
Right: More motorized units after the Germans crossed the Marne at Château-Thierry on 12 June.
Below: A German patrol looks out for snipers in Atigny.
Below right: A German propaganda poster in France shows the advance by the end of May.

Above: Marshal Philippe Pétain, who took power over the Third Republic in its final days.

ing the Retourne. Once more the hedgehogs came into the conflict, and it was not until midafternoon that these had been silenced. Guderian pressed on with his advance, but was caught up in an armored battle when a French Group under Buisson, waiting for his flank, came on the scene. Unfortunately they were too late and could do little to turn the tide of battle. Such successes as they achieved were largely local ones, nullified and forgotten as the real struggle followed its destined course.

Guderian's 1st Panzer Division was followed across the river by his 2nd which had swung left and by the afternoon of that day was at Reims, capital of Champagne and once the crowning place of kings, pushing the Sixth Army toward the Marne. The Fourth Army on its left, outflanked, had to abandon its line on the Aisne at Rethel, though it managed to keep contact with the Sixth and Second Armies on either side. However, exhausted by resistance against such great odds and having suffered severe casualties, it was incapable of further organized resistance. By the next night Reims had fallen and the enemy was advancing on Fourth Army's line.

River lines, which earlier in the war had seemed to hold out so much hope, were proving themselves less and less capable of providing any sort of obstacle at all to the enemy's advance. It was, no doubt,

**Left: German infantry crouch in a bunker near the Aisne in early June.
Below left: Exhausted Germans pause for a breather on the road to Paris.
Below center: German artillery in action near the Aisne.
Below: French girl fraternizes with German troops near the Aisne.
Overleaf: The ruins of a French town on the Oise River.**

because the exercise of destroying bridges had come to seem so pointless that the Germans found more and more of them left standing and because of this the Panzers were now able to pour over the Seine and Marne, bringing Paris even closer to the front line. Again the recollections of World War I were aired. On the 3rd it was bombed and there were many who recalled this had happened before. The only difference was that the raider then was a single *Taube* whose pilot threw his handfuls of explosive over the side of his cockpit. Now it was wave upon wave of bombers. By the 8th the sound of gunfire was audible within the city walls, though some stalwarts recalled that 'it had been the same in 1914.' But the government had finally decided there was going to be no victory of the Marne in this war and left, while GHQ was evacuated to Briare on the lower Loire. De Gaulle

Above: The partition of France.
Right: Germans guard the Gare de
l'Est in Paris on 14 June 1940.
Below: German troops line up for
inspection at Versailles.
Opposite: The final stages of
Blitzkrieg 1940.

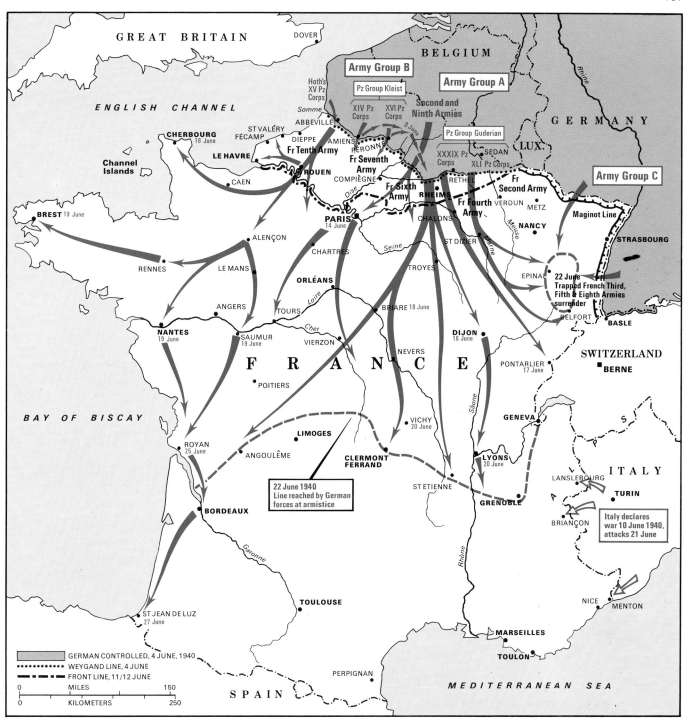

recalls the fast cars, racing down the *Routes Nationales*, their chauffeurs keeping up a constant fanfare on their horns as they flew past the long, dejected lines of refugees. Within the city itself, the railway stations were packed almost to the point of immobility as people tried to find places in trains which might take them a little further from the place where the armies were locked in struggle — at least for a time.

On 11 June, to prevent the loveliest of European cities from suffering the fate of Rotterdam, Paris was declared an open city and all troops and guns removed from its precincts. The excuse given by the government and general staff for their abandonment of the city was that it was necessary in order to continue the prosecution of the war. The reality was that they were bankrupt of ideas as to how the war was to be prosecuted. For

Weygand it had been prolonged uselessly in any case. He had been in favor of capitulation the moment his Somme line was breached. Now his imagination could take him no further than some sort of massive retreat, a heroic struggle to the last man who, presumably, would have died walking backwards.

On the morning of 11 June, the day Paris was declared an open city and the day after the armies had suffered so terribly, Weygand did his stocktaking. There were fifty-two divisions left, although combat losses had reduced the strength of these to nearly the equivalent of thirty full-strength ones. Another disadvantage was that they were dispersed with great gaps driven through them so that they were out of contact with one another. All in all they amounted more to pockets of continuing resistance than to a front.

That same day Weygand issued the plans for his retreat, though not yet the orders for its execution. The movement was intended to take the armies back to a crescent-shaped line running from Caen in Normandy through to the Jura. Along it were to be spread four Armies: the Tenth, Army Group 3, which included the Paris and Seventh Armies, Army Group 4 and Army Group 2, including troops from the Maginot Line.

In the evening Churchill paid his first visit to the new GHQ at Briare, taking Eden with him, while Weygand was accompanied by Pétain. The first was sunk in gloom, the hero of Verdun in apathy. There was little hope that a new line could be held, even assuming the order was given to take it up and that the Armies successfully did so. The whole of France was about to be engulfed. De Gaulle saw the meeting as mere 'palaver.'

The only workable solution was for the Armies to position themselves so they could hold out until help reached them from across the sea. In other words, they needed to hold a bridgehead with a shortened line.

The following day witnessed still further deterioration. Paris was still unoccupied, but, as most people who were there at the time recall, it was a ghost city. There had, however, been advances in the lower Seine region, across the Marne where Montmirail, headquarters of the Sixth Army, was reached, and through Champagne heading toward Châlons. As he was later to write with the perverse delight of the congenital pessimist who sees his worst forecasts realized, Weygand saw everywhere the defense lines cracking, disruption, dislocation, defeat – *toute est dégradation*.

All the same, he felt able to write, 'My resolve was unshakably formed!' Brave words. Until one reached the next: 'In a few hours I should ask the government to conclude an armistice.' Some soldiers

Left: The advance guard of the German victory parade at the Arc de Triomphe, Place de l'Etoile.
Right: Occupying Germans pass the Cathedral of Notre-Dame.
Below: Germans bivouac in the Place Royale, Paris in front of the Louvre department store.

The Capitulation at Compiègne

The German surrender in 1918 was signed in a railway carriage at Compiègne north of Paris. Hitler and Goebbels decided it would be fitting if the French surrender in 1940 took place in the same carriage at the same location.

1 The carriage is taken from its museum to be placed where it had been situated in 1918.
2 The historic carriage is taken from its place in Paris to Compiègne.
3 The deliberations in the carriage prior to the armistice.
4 The carriage on the morning of the surrender, 22 June.
5 The French delegation moves ominously toward the carriage.
6 General von Brauchitsch, Admiral Raeder, Hitler, Hess, Göring, von Ribbentrop and aides Schmundt and Brückner.
7 The French and German delegations meet before they enter the historic railway car.
8 The French leave the carriage after the surrender: Vice-Admiral Le Luc, Air Force General Bergeret, General Huntziger and M Léon Noël.

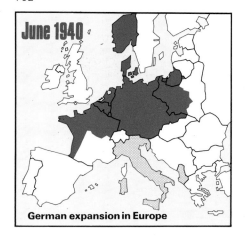

June 1940

German expansion in Europe

have been criticized for not knowing when they were beaten. None could make so unjust an accusation against the Commander in Chief of the French Armies in June 1940. His nose for defeat was unfailing.

The continuation of the war had now become a side issue. Weygand had told the armies where to retreat. From now on he was wholly exercised with his endeavors to persuade the government to make peace.

On 13 June it looked as if Paris was soon to be occupied as the enemy forces crossed the Seine to the west, took Evreux and began advancing toward Dreux. The Tenth Army, pushed before it, made for Brittany. That day, too, Army Group 3 left its positions in front of the capital as the first stage in a move to a line from Rambouillet to Corbeil.

No one could now pretend France possessed anything resembling a cohesive force. Communications, always bad, were now almost nonexistent. Orders failed to reach their destination because those who bore them could not get through the columns of refugees.

Constantly under attack, the men were exhausted to paralysis and were strafed every time they moved; losses were to be counted not only in the fallen, but also in those who had simply dropped out of the fight! Each time a unit was ordered to make a stand, its will was sapped by rumors of encirclement which all too often turned out to be well founded.

Next day, the 14th, the Germans began entering Paris, the City of Light, at first moving suspiciously as if it were a trap, but then with advancing confidence as they realized it was not.

Above left: Europe after 1940.
Above: German troops at the Place de l'Opéra.

There were few to greet them; handfuls of the curious idled on street corners, here and there a man or a woman wept, but for most of the day, the people remained within closed doors.

The day after came a symbolically important event: Verdun was captured. Panzer commanders crowed that they had achieved what months of struggle and hundreds of thousands of the dead had failed to achieve in 1916. This time

Below: Germans mingle with French civilians at St Ouen.
Right: A convoy of French prisoners of war passes through the Place de l'Opéra in Paris.

the cost was twenty-four hours fighting and 200 dead.

It could truly be said that now all remaining for the Germans was pursuit, and orders for this were issued that same day. The remaining defenders had to be rounded up; in particular there was the need to prevent the sanctuary of the Maginot Line from being reached. And now it had its brief day of glory. Surrounded, the troglodytes within fought as their fathers had in the fortresses of Verdun. They were still fighting when the battle of France ended and had to be sent a special message by Weygand to give up.

Elsewhere, Bordeaux, Dijon, Lyon, the 'Torres Vedras' of Brittany were under threat, but this was all aftermath. The real battle as everyone, friend and foe alike, sensed had been lost and won. The XVI Panzer Corps was even dispatched southward to help the Italians in the Alpine passes.

An effort was made to organize retreat, to regroup, to bring about cohesion. It had little hope of success; every kind of detour was sought to avoid contact with the enemy, but the Germans were invariably found to have preceded, with their motorized forces, the slower moving French ones. Still the attempts, often unbelievably valiant, were made. On the 15th the Third, Fifth and Eighth Armies tried to concentrate in the Vosges. They held out for a week before being authorized by Weygand to surrender. That day

400,000 men fell into the Germans' net.

And it was at this moment that the Italians, who had been massing along the French border in the south, struck with thirty-two divisions against the six French ones holding the Alpine Front under General Olry. In fact the defenders proved more than enough. The Italians mounted assault after assault, but failed to penetrate

Above: The honor guard passes in the victory parade down the Avenue Foch leading to the Place de l'Etoile.
Above right: Weary German troops after the long parade of triumph.
Right: A German soldier watches a French village burn.
Below: The victory parade.

except locally. In one place a single non-commissioned officer (NCO) with seven men successfully held, then turned back the divisions of the invaders.

It was not until the Germans could take the Alpine divisions holding the passes from the rear that a real opportunity was opened for the Italians. Even then it was little enough, for here a French force hurriedly sent to the area under General Cartier held out in Grenoble until the armistice.

It was armistice which had become the principal concern. In particular the commanders were anxious to prevent Reynaud from carrying out his own plan to move government, the navy and as much as possible of the army to North Africa to

**Left: German artillery parades down the Champs Elysées.
Below: The parade down the Boulevard Haussmann.
Right: A German cemetery in France.**

The victory parade down the
Avenue Foch.

Right: The German victory parade passes the Place de la Concorde.

continue the struggle. This, they believed, would infuriate Hitler and make his terms more punitive. Determined and courageous, Reynaud had so far refused all their blandishments.

On 16 June the Cabinet met. Pétain tried to force the issue by tendering his resignation, but agreed to withdraw it as the government was waiting for an answer to an appeal it had addressed to the President of the United States seeking an immediate American intervention. (It was refused.) Reynaud then referred to a proposal for political union between France and Britain. Ironically enough in the light of subsequent events, the suggestion conveyed to Reynaud by Churchill had actually originated in French minds and had the support of de Gaulle. It was turned down speedily enough. Britain was about to be beaten, Pétain predicted. He had no wish to unite with a corpse. Instead a majority appeared to favor another course, which was to ask the Germans their conditions for an armistice. This, Reynaud believed, was simply temporizing and finding himself overruled on all counts, he resigned.

Pétain had been hankering for just such an opportunity. For days he had been carrying in his pocket the names of men who would form his new government, one ready to treat with the enemy. He had already told one government minister that he was not at all afraid of meeting Hitler. He would approach him as one soldier to another.

That day the man he would so gladly have met ordered his Panzers to push toward Cherbourg and Brest. The next day, Rennes, capital of Brittany, fell, and with it the headquarters of the Tenth Army. The peninsula, once conceived of as the bridgehead for the continuance of the struggle, was now itself about to fall. Elsewhere there was some resistance along the Loire, particularly in the Tours/Saumur region.

At 2200 on the night of the 16th, Reynaud went to Lebrun, the President of the Republic, and told him of his resignation. Pétain was summoned immediately and read through his list of Cabinet members. The first meeting was called forthwith and in ten minutes had authorized Paul Baudouin, Minister of Foreign Affairs, to ask the Germans and the Italians for armistice terms, going via Madrid and the Vatican respectively.

The move had by no means found the Germans unprepared; two days before, on

Left: German artillery and French refugees on the Place de la Concorde.
Right: The Germans occupy a German-speaking town in the province of Lorraine.

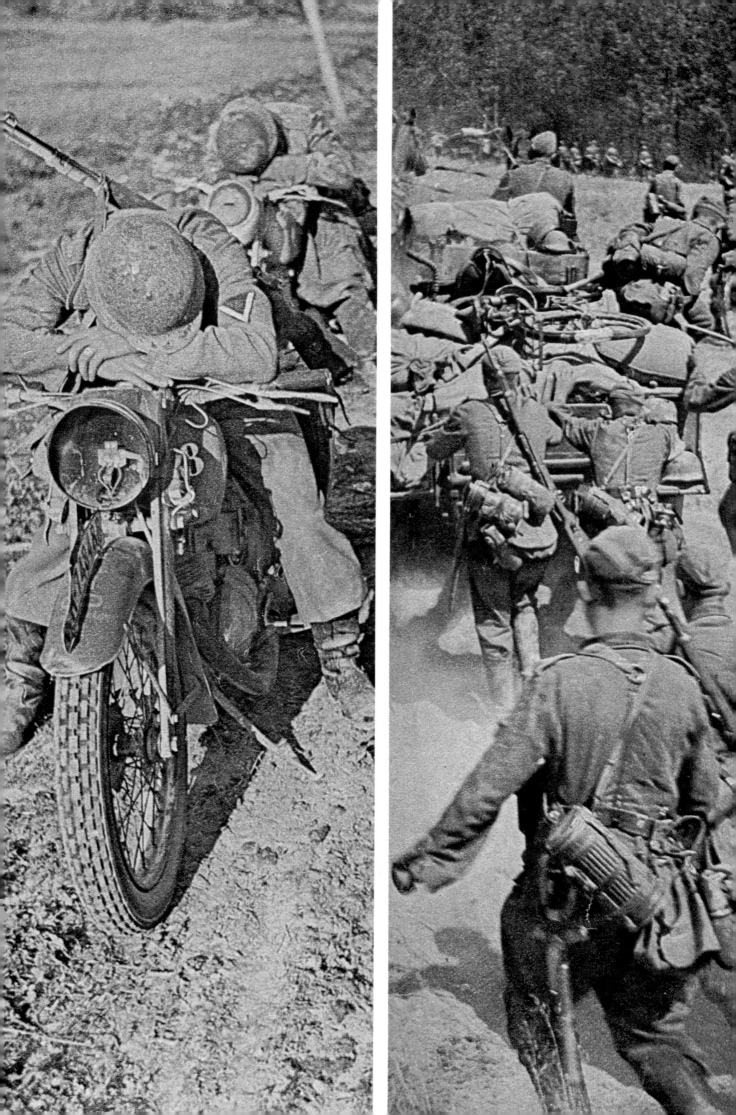

Opposite: Advance and rest; the race to occupy France exhausted both the men and their supply lines. Above: French civilians and German troops at the victory parade in Paris. Left: The horse cavalry trumpets the arrival of the victorious German armies on the Champs Elysées.

the 15th, a draft armistice convention had been drawn up at OKH. When news of the French feelers reached him, Hitler decided its terms were too humiliating. It was better to offer them something which the French people would find more acceptable. In that way Germany could obtain, as a *quid pro quo*, a complete breach with Britain and the handing over of the fleet and what remained of the air force, thus preventing their transfer to North Africa. This required that some part of France remain in being, a skeleton, to prevent the colonial empire from joining in resistance.

On the 19th Germany announced its readiness to present terms. The following day the French sent the list of plenipotentiaries to participate in what were then thought to be negotiations. That afternoon they left Bordeaux upon which the Germans were advancing. There were no negotiations. The French delegation was simply handed the convention and told they had until 1930 to sign it or be returned to their army's outposts.

At 1842, having telephoned Bordeaux, they did so. It was not quite the end of the struggle, since another convention had to be signed with the Italians in Rome. In view of the successes of the French Army against those of Mussolini, this was a final humiliation and even the Italian representatives seemed apologetic. At 0135 on the 25th, hostilities ceased. That day Pétain declared in a broadcast to the nation, 'Honor is saved! . . . A new order is beginning.'

The interpretation which men like Weygand and Pétain gave to the word 'honor' sometimes seems a trifle arbitrary to lesser mortals. The former had once spoken of having 'the ghastly job of meeting the Germans, just as at Rethondes.' It all turned out just as he had predicted — with an exact reversal of roles. The Germans even went to the trouble of having the railway carriage in which the 1918 Armistice had been signed brought from the museum that housed it so that the Führer could sit there in triumph to witness the act of revenge, the *Vergeltung* he had so long promised, in its achievement. It had not, however, been Weygand who had had 'the ghastly job.' That had fallen to the lot of one of his generals, Huntziger. He was a brave and resourceful man, yet it was perhaps not totally unfitting that he should have been chosen: he had been in command that dreadful day at Sedan when the Panzers broke through.

The graves of five Wehrmacht soldiers who would not be able to celebrate the German victory.

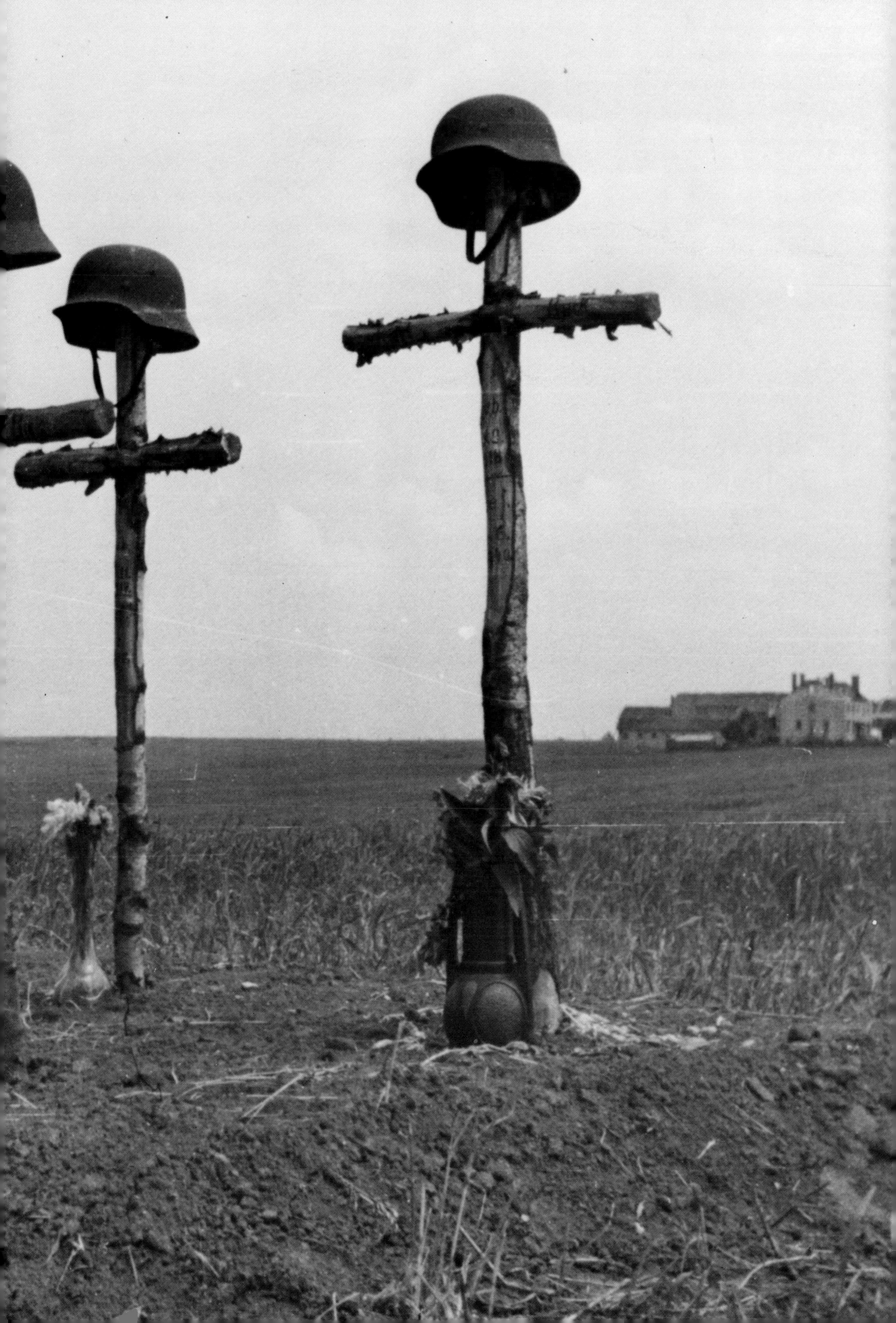

WHY FR

Hitler at the foot of the Eiffel Tower.

ANCE FELL

The campaign in the west had resulted in the defeat of the armies of two great nations such as has rarely been known to military history. Not surprisingly it was duly celebrated in Germany, among other ways in the documentary *Sieg im Westen* (Victory in the West) produced by Goebbels' *Propaganda Kompanien*.

Disregarding the element of luck on the German side — and this was considerable — one automatically asks how did such a situation occur. The answer comes as a confused babble of voices, shrill with complaining. Certainly the legacy of the war was suspicion and recrimination between France and Britain which has lasted down to our own times. When, in the fifties, Eden turned down out of hand the invitation for Britain to join the nascent European Economic Community, he was undoubtedly thinking of his countrymen's feelings toward those with whom they would have to be intimately associated. It was the same kind of consideration which activated de Gaulle when, later, he vetoed the belated British attempts to join.

Both remembered 1940. France, the one side says, caved in, leaving Britain to fight alone; and on the other side it is said that Britain dragged France into war and then ran away.

The facts of history are that Britain entered the war with its greatest ally a European power. It ended the war with its greatest ally the transatlantic one. It was another alliance filled with difficulty, yet the British gave every indication of preferring it and the 'special relationship' was born. Britain had broken with Europe, the continent to which it was geographically joined and was never again to show any real desire to rejoin it. Not for the first time in her history, Britain had judged Europe and found her wanting.

In this case, it was nonetheless a premature and biassed verdict. Given that there was sufficient demoralization in the French Army to daunt the staunchest ally and that the country had gone to war over a place it knew little and cared less about; given that there was defeatism in high places and many believed that to weaken Hitler was to strengthen Stalin; given that it is a truism of war that one does not invest in failure and the French Army's showing had largely been one of failure — one has also to realize that the France of 1940 also contained many brave, able and patriotic officers — de Gaulle, Giraud, de Lattre de Tassigny and Prioux to name a few. France also had many units which fought with self-sacrificial gallantry, as at Dunkirk, to save an ally. Is there not something undignified and witless about the continuation of wartime grudges, which can be compared to two old men keeping up the quarrel of their boyhood?

If there were errors, then these can be equally apportioned. At a meeting on 11 June between Churchill and Reynaud at which Weygand was present, the French premier once more pressed his

Right: The debris of Dunkirk, taken from the German propaganda film *Sieg im Westen*, which was made after the Fall of France.
Below: A British troopship returns to England with RAF officers and men aboard.

country's need for air support. His British partner promised to do what he could, insisting that the decisive battle would be the one over England. Reynaud, seeing this as tantamount to refusal, commented, 'No doubt history will say the Battle of France was lost through lack of aircraft.'

Below: Generalissimo Francisco Franco, who met Hitler on the Spanish border after the Fall of France.

'And through lack of tanks,' Churchill countered. Significantly Weygand's account includes Reynaud's remark and omits the rejoinder to it. What is not taken into account is that France herself had started off the war with an Air Force infinitely larger than the RAF and had frittered it away. At the same time Churchill's answer can also be turned back on him. Britain had provided all too few tanks and these were mostly inadequate to their task.

The roots of the dispute lie in the inflexible minds of military commanders, British and French, and then in the panic which ensued when their miscalculations had their effects – a panic felt more potently in France which was being invaded, than in Britain. Such miscalculations were not unfamiliar. In 1904 war broke out between Russia and Japan. The Western nations sent their military observers to witness what was in fact the first modern war. Most of them reported back on the devastating combination of machine guns and barbed wire they had seen and at least one, Colonel Max Hoffman of the German General Staff, predicted that trench-warfare was going to be the pattern of the future. He and his colleagues of France and Britain alike were ignored by their superiors. The Russo-Japanese War was 'the exception that proved the rule' – the rule that wars were always fought the same way, by

Above: Bedraggled remnants of the once-proud BEF arrive home.

moving and maneuvering bodies of troops.

In time the union of tank and aircraft in Spain, then in Poland, were shown to be 'exceptions.' For the second time in twenty-five years France prepared for the wrong war. Insofar as Britain prepared, it had done likewise. Fortunately it had hardly prepared at all, which operated to its advantage in the long run, for having gained the necessary respite, it was able to design its arsenal to meet the challenge.

It should not be forgotten that Britain was granted this respite very largely because the French Army held out for six precious weeks. In the three months April, May and June 1940, British aircraft production totalled 3851, compared with 2381 in the previous three months. In fighter production, the comparison is even more dramatic: from 477 turned out in January, February and March to 1027 in April, May and June. It was this which enabled the RAF to win the Battle of Britain.

It also provides part of the answer to one French criticism. 'Why should the Luftwaffe not have been defeated on French soil?' Weygand asks. The answer is that for most of the Battle of France, British air strength was simply insufficient.

In any case, to destroy an enemy one must first know where he is and then be able to get to him. This was true during the Battle of Britain where Dowding was able to make such accurate estimates of the probable enemy targets and organize his defenses within reach of them. In the fluid struggle in France this was impossible, as the French Air Force learned to its cost.

At the same time there is little doubt that a bigger British bomber force in France, used in close co-operation with the troops on the ground and perhaps pre-empting the unnerving Stuka attacks, would probably have achieved far more than was achieved in other ways. The RAF bombing attacks on Germany were almost totally ineffective. They did not result in enemy fighters being taken from the battle line and so had no effect on the outcome of the struggle. Letters written by Germans in the places attacked speak of desultory British raids and even of bombs which failed to detonate. All too often it was not missiles the planes dropped, but leaflets filled with the most puerile propaganda.

For all this wasted effort the British were validly criticized by the French, as they were for the fact that the so-called Air Component of the BEF was recalled to Britain so early in the struggle.

Undoubtedly one of the factors in its defeat was that in 1939 France was (and still is) a fundamentally divided country. Its 'haves' regarded the retention of power and possession as more important than fighting a war which they believed would merely ensure their loss; its 'have-nots' saw the 'haves' as the real enemy.

Sir Edward Spears, who before being appointed Churchill's representative with Reynaud because of his knowledge and love of France, was a Conservative member of the House of Commons. Even he was constrained to write of 'the merciless attitude of the property-owning, particularly industrial classes, the *patrons* (bosses).' British officers found incomprehensible and damnable the arrogant disdain which so many of their French counterparts showed toward the ordinary *poilu* and his well-being. This very considerably affected the men's fighting morale.

As a very broad, and in some ways unfair, generalization one can say that the French Army contained a sizeable minority of officers who felt they had more in common with the German National Socialists than with many people in their own government. Equally, it contained another sizeable minority of men imbued with the notion that they were being dragged into an imperialist war. There were, besides, a great proportion of men who thought the reasons for going to war totally insufficient, particularly after Poland's capitulation.

In these circumstances it was no wonder that there was a reluctance to antagonize the enemy, to spur him to

reprisal. The only interruption in the 'Phony War' before May 1940 was the 'Phony Offensive' in the Saar. When Churchill suggested the idea of floating mines down the Rhine to disrupt Germany's important river shipping, it was quietly allowed to drop. The RAF crews in France, preparing for bombing missions were frequently stopped by the local governments in the area they were stationed for fear of retaliatory action. When the enemy attacked, gasoline supplies, vital for his Panzers, were allowed to fall into his hands undestroyed; bridges were left spanning rivers so that they could cross; in some instances armed civilians even shot at their own troops.

The British have themselves to blame, too. Had they shown a more aggressive spirit, had they been less dilatory in sending troops across the Channel, had they given any sort of impression they could defend the people in whose country they were fighting, French morale, civilian and military, might well have

Above: Anti-British posters put up in Paris after the surrender. The French felt deeply let down.

improved. As it was, German propaganda made great play of the absence of the British in persuading the French troops it was they who were going to do the fighting. We know, too, what answer was given when it was suggested that the RAF attack the German arms stores in the Black Forest.

In contrast with all this half-hearted behavior on the Allied side, there was the vigorous and determined action of the German attackers. These combined with the terrifying weapons they employed and, one can say, their free use of terror methods, such as the bombing of Rotterdam, contributed to the speedy victory.

There was one other factor, to which

Below: Hitler and von Ribbentrop greet Marshal Pétain, who took control of Vichy France.

too scant attention has been paid. In contrast with the methods used to win victory were the men who won it — the German soldiers who began to stream in, the victors personified. It seems almost perverse, remembering the horrors like those of Oradour sur Glâne, to suggest that the men of Hitler's armies were actually preferable to those of the Kaiser's. Yet such was the case. I have yet to meet anyone who, having experienced German occupation in both world wars, did not agree that the men of 1940 were infinitely preferable to their fathers. Well-

disciplined, courteous and friendly, they were soon fraternizing with the people of places they occupied. Even the most die-hard anti-German had to agree that their behavior was 'correct.' Spears, quoting reports he had received, describes the reception given to the Germans as they arrived in a French village he knew. Its people were awakened by the rumble of tanks; at first frightened, they gradually became curious and went to windows to observe. Soon all were full. As they saw them the German soldiers waved, blew kisses to the girls who occasionally waved or laughed back their response.

Rommel speaks of troops passing through the country and coming across peasants calmly working in the field. The soldiers, often countrymen too, would stop and talk; sometimes they even found time to strip off their uniform jacket and help. Of course, it did not continue so amicably. There were the repressive laws of the military government, the brutal racial measures, the sinister, omnipresent

**Far left: Hitler greets Premier Pierre Laval of Vichy France.
Left: Franco greets Hitler at Biarritz near the Spanish border.
Below left: Ambassador Kurusu, Count Ciano and Hitler listen as Foreign Minister von Ribbentrop announces the Tripartite Pact.
Below: President Pétain, Admiral Darlan and Premier Laval.**

Gestapo and its network of torturers, the hostages and sickening printed posters with their lists of the newly executed which were to be found in the tiniest hamlet. But all this, as most French people would explain, came 'from the top,' not from the men in field-gray in their midst.

It is true to say that the Nazi leaders made a real effort to treat the captive peoples of Scandinavia, the Low Countries and France with infinitely more courtesy than the peoples of Eastern Europe who were, after all, Slavs. The racist doctrine which the Nazis espoused suggested, and the Nazi leaders demanded, that 'Aryans' be treated as brothers in the struggle against the 'sub-human,' non-Aryan peoples of Europe. For that reason, hoping to gain support among the states they had just conquered, the Third Reich behaved 'correctly' — at least for a while. And the Nazis received both tacit and active support from a shamefully large number of Dutch, Belgians and French, certainly during the first two years of the occupation.

One is forced to wonder what would have been the effect if the Germans had behaved with similar 'correctness' in Russia? Perhaps we should be thankful that their conduct there made it so easy for Stalin to demand of his people a 'Patriotic War' against atrociously blood-thirsty invaders, truly 'the barbarians from the west.'

All these, then, are factors which led to the German success. They are all part of that succession of events which made the war into the long, tedious procession of suffering beginning in Danzig and ending in Nagasaki. Yet this still omits the fundamental factor — the two great follies of the British and French. The first was to give a worthless guarantee to Poland and the second was to pretend to keep it.

Above: General Charles de Gaulle, leader of the Free French.
Right: A French soldier surrendered.
Far right: Paris, July 1940.
Overleaf: The smile of success as the victorious German troops parade through Berlin.

INDEX

Acknowledgments

Designer: David Eldred.
Editor: Catherine Bradley.
Cartographer: Richard Natkiel.
Picture researchers: Rolf Steinberg and
Catherine Bradley.

The author and publisher would like to
thank the following libraries which
supplied pictures:
Bison Picture Library: pp 10 (top),
11 (bottom), 12–13, 17, 22 (bottom),
25, 27 (bottom left), 28–29, 28 (top
right), 29 (top), 30, 31 (top), 32–33,
34–35, 36, 42–43, 49, 52–53, 54, 56
(top), 57 (top), 60 (top), 64 (top left),
98, 99, 100, 101 (top and bottom left),
102–103, 104–105 (top three), 106–
107, 108–109, 110–111 (top), 114–
115, 118–119 (bottom), 120–121

(below), 133 (bottom), 136 (top), 137,
138, 139 (top), 153 (top), 165, 167
(top), 168–169, 171 (bottom), 172,
173 (bottom), 180 (bottom), 181, 182
(top), 183, 184.
Bundesarchiv: pp 8–9, 10 (bottom),
11 (inset), 14–15, 16, 18–19, 19 (top),
23, 24, 27 (bottom left), 28 (top left),
31 (below), 72, 84, 86–87, 90–91,
92–93, 94–95, 96–97, 101 (bottom
right), 105 (below), 112–113 (bottom),
113 (top and center left), 118–119 (top
three), 122–123 (bottom), 128–129,
130–131 (top), 133 (top), 134–135,
136 (bottom), 139 (bottom), 148 (top),
149 (bottom), 150, 151, 152 (top),
152–153 (bottom), 154–155, 156, 158–
159, 160, 161, 162–163, 164, 166 (top),
166–167, 170, 173 (top), 174–175,

176–177, 182 (bottom), 185.
Imperial War Museum: pp 6–7, 26,
27 (top), 68–69, 73, 74–75, 76–77,
78–79, 80, 82–83, 84 (top), 89 (top),
110–111 (bottom), 112 (top), 113
(center right), 120 (top), 121 (top),
122 (top), 123 (top three), 124
(bottom), 125, 126, 127, 130–131
(bottom), 140–141, 144–145, 146–147,
148 (bottom), 149 (top), 170 (top),
178–179, 180 (top).
**Rijksinstituut voor Oorlogsdocu-
mentatie, Amsterdam:** pp 38–39,
46–47, 48, 56–57 (bottom), 58–59,
60–61, 62–63, 64 (top left), 65, 66–67,
84 (bottom).
Popperfoto: p 18 (top).

Bibliography

Benoist-Machine, J, ed Cyril Falls, *Sixty Days that Shook the West.*

Bryant, Sir Arthur, *The Turn of the Tide, 1939–43.*

Belgium: The Official Account of What Happened, 1939–40.

Churchill, Winston L S, *The Second World War,* Vol II, *Their Finest Hour*

Colville, J R, *Man of Valour: Field Marshal Lord Gort*

Divine, David, *The Nine Days of Dunkirk*

Ellis, L, *The War in France and Flanders, 1939–40*

Fabribecker, E, *La Campagne de l'Armée Belge en 1940*

Fuller, Major General, J F C, *Decisive Battles of the Western World,* Vol III

Gamelin, General M, *Servir,* Vols II and III

de Gaulle, Charles, trs, Griffin, *War Memoirs,* Vol I

Goutard, Colonel Adolphe, *The Fall of France*

Guderian, Colonel General Heinz, trs, Fitzgibbon, *Panzer Leader*

L'Hoest, J-L, *Les Paras Allemands au Canal Albert, Mai 1940*

Horne, Alistair, *To Lose a Battle*

Ironside Diaries, The, eds Roderick and Denis Kelly

Kennedy, John F, *Why England Slept*

Kleffens, E N van, *The Rape of the Netherlands*

Liddell Hart, Captain Sir Basil, *The Tanks,* Vol I and II

Liddell Hart, Captain Sir Basil, *The Rommel Papers*

Macksey, Kenneth, *Armoured Crusader*

Manstein, Field Marshal Erich von, *Lost Victories*

Maurois, André, *Why France Fell*

Mellenthin, Major General F W von, *Panzer Battles, 1939–45,* ed L C F Turner

Michiels, O, *Dix-Huit Jours de Guerre en Belgique*

Montgomery of Alamein, Field Marshal the Viscount, *Memoirs*

Ogorkiewicz, R, *Armour*

Spears, Major General Sir Edward, *Prelude to Dunkirk, July 1939–May 1940*

Warlimont, General W, *Inside Hitler's Headquarters*

Weygand, General M, *Rappèle au Service*

Young, Desmond, *Rommel*